# The Rosary

••••

# The NEW Loveful Mysteries, Meditation Beads, and More.

# The Rosary
●●●●
## *The NEW Loveful Mysteries,*
## *Meditation Beads,*
## *and More.*

For publication of this book, the author relies on Canon
827 §3 [1983].
Except as otherwise noted, all scriptural quotes are from the
New Catholic Bible (NCB). Quotes from the Catechism of the
Catholic Church are from its 2nd Edition, December 2020
printing.
Cover photo© shows a rosary with a Meditation Bead added
to each of the five decades. Chapter Three has details.

*Paperback edition:*
ISBN: 978-1-878038-02-9
*Published in the United States of America.    (121224)*
*No artificial intelligence was used in the writing of this
book.*™

*Multi-Services Publishing Company • Since 1989*
*contact@multiservicespublishing.com*
*multiservicespublishing.com*

*As is the case with all technology, digital resources,
including websites, are always temporary.*

# DEDICATION

*This Book Is Dedicated*
*To My Mother,*
*who made me a Catholic.*

•••••••••••••

*And In Memory of*
*Joyce Ann Drake (1958–2016),*
*of the Diocese of San Bernardino, California,*
*whose journey to Catholicism*
*made me a Catholic — again.*
*As of this writing, her cause for*
*sainthood has not yet begun.*

# Meditations on Love and the Rosary

**(Part 1)** These first meditations are from St. Bernard of Clairvaux:

*"Love is sufficient of itself; it gives pleasure by itself and because of itself. It is its own merit, its own reward. Love looks for no cause outside itself, no effect beyond itself...*

•••••

*"Of all the movements, sensations, and feelings of the soul, love is the only one in which the creature can respond to the Creator and make some sort of similar return however unequal though it be. For when God loves, all he desires is to be loved in return. The sole purpose of his love is to be loved, in the knowledge that those who love him are made happy by their love of him."*

•••••

"The reason for loving God is God Himself. The measure is to love Him beyond measure."

[Those meditations were from St. Bernard of Clairvaux.]

## (Part 2)
As part of her September 25, 2019 message from Medjugorje, Our Lady said:[1]

*"Little children, pray the Rosary and meditate [on] the mysteries of the Rosary because, in your life, you are also passing through joys and sorrows. In this way, you are transforming the mysteries into your life, because life is a mystery until you place it into God's hands. In this way, you will have the experience of faith like Peter who met Jesus and the Holy Spirit filled his heart."*

---

[1] *See the* Preface *regarding events in Medjugorje.*

## PREFACE

For many years, apparitions of Our Lady have been reported at Medjugorje in Bosnia-Herzegovina. Numerous messages from Medjugorje are referenced in this book in whole or in part. Therefore, a few words regarding Medjugorje and the messages from there is important as we begin.

Although the Loveful Mysteries are not from or part of the apparitions at Medjugorje, quotes from the messages given by Our Lady at those apparitions help us to better understand Our Lady's teachings on the importance of love. In September 2024, the Vatican's Dicastery for the Doctrine of the Faith, released a *"Note About the Spiritual Experience Connected with Medjugorje."* It was approved and signed by Pope Francis.

The Note says that *"... the faithful can receive a positive encouragement for their Christian life through this spiritual proposal and it authorizes public acts of devotion"* regarding Medjugorje.

Combined with earlier approvals permitting church-sponsored pilgrimages, and the placement of an archbishop as the officially appointed "Apostolic Visitor" assigned indefinitely for the parish of Medjugorje,[2] all even before the recent Note, it is clear that the Catholic Church his shown itself positively inclined towards the many fruits found at and through the events at Medjugorje.

The Note also gives support for the countless messages coming from Medjugorje. Although some few messages have needed clarification regarding certain expressions, the vast majority of messages from the reported apparitions there have not needed such clarifications.

There are plenty of books, videos, and websites available in order to learn the full story and messages of Our Lady's apparitions, both in Medjugorje and elsewhere. Among a number of other websites, you can go directly to the site for Medjugorje at: medjugorje.hr/en or to www.medjugorje.org.

---

[2] *As per medjugorje.org, accessed Jan 12, 2022.*

I have personal experience related to the events there and take the position that the events and messages from Medjugorje should indeed be taken seriously.

*But again, other than the messages, nothing in this book has come directly from Medjugorje.*

Rosarycenter.org is a source for even more information on the Rosary. There, you'll also find information on the Rosary Confraternity.

But also note that the Loveful Mysteries, along with other materials in this book, are not connected to the Rosary Center, the Dominicans, or authors of any quoted sources. Any websites listed here were accessible at the time of this writing. As with all technology, future access to websites cannot be guaranteed.

This book is written primarily for Roman Catholics who pray the Rosary. Therefore, it makes assumptions of understanding that some others may not have. Nonetheless, it is believed that others may benefit, too. Those who do not know how to pray the Rosary will find help to learn this powerful prayer in the appendices to this book.

Parts of this book are based on a series of talks given by the author in 2021.

L.S.Scarpitta

•••••••••

A note on capitalization: In this, as well as in other books, the term Rosary is capitalized when it refers to the actual Rosary *prayer(s)*. It is lowercase when it refers to the *beads*, to the physical rosary itself.

## TABLE OF CONTENTS

# CHAPTER ONE

## The Rosary's Missing History;
## An Attack on The Rosary;
## No Time For God?

## THE BEGINNING

In Medjugorje, Our Lady has said that the Mass is the best prayer.

Next to the Mass is the Rosary.[3]

*Continuing what was begun in the Preface, the reported apparitions of Our Lady to six visionaries at Medjugorje began in June 1981. They continue at the time of this writing. Despite positive reporting by some of the largest news media organizations in the early years of this event, and despite millions of people who have visited and continue to visit, many people are still not even aware of what has been happening there. If you are one, please visit one of the websites listed in the* Preface *at the front of this book, or read one of the many books available on the apparitions. Books written in the early years of the apparitions are especially recommended by the author. Medjugorje is located in the country of Bosnia and Herzegovina, south of Croatia, in Southeastern Europe. Other than the messages, nothing in this book has come directly from Medjugorje.[4]*

In this book, we will find out about the new Loveful Mysteries. We will then look at Meditation Beads. They can help those who have trouble staying focused while praying the

---

[3] *The preeminence of the Mass was made clear in Our Lady's messages at Medjugorje. (The Eucharist was directly given to us by Jesus at the Last Supper.) As just three examples from messages at Medjugorje: "Let Holy Mass be your life (4-25-1988)." "May Holy Mass, little children, not be a habit for you, but life (1-25-1998)." "May the Mass, the most exalted and most powerful act of your prayer, be the center of your spiritual life (8-2-2008)." See the Preface regarding the events and messages from Medjugorje.*

[4] *Although the author has visited Medjugorje, it was while in America that the author personally witnessed what appeared to be supernatural events related to the apparitions. Those include a rosary, not my own, appearing to turn a golden color while in my hand within a Medjugorje context — and a seemingly miraculous event involving the sun.*

Rosary. Finally, we'll look at some common elements connecting some of the Rosary's mysteries.

I recommend beginning with Chapter One. But, if your interest is only in the Loveful Mysteries (Chapter Two) or the Meditation Beads (Chapter Three), you can skip forward to those chapters.

In this first chapter, we'll start by trying to find the Rosary's history. You can choose the shorter version or the longer one. We'll then look at how some non-Catholics mistakenly view the Rosary. Finally, we'll consider where our time for God has gone. If the surprising history of the Rosary holds no interest for you, feel free to skip ahead three sections to *Going Beyond History*.

There are three important appendices at the back of the book for you. In them, you'll find:

Appendix A: Mysteries of the Rosary;

Appendix B: How To Pray The Rosary; and

Appendix C: Prayers of the Rosary.

## A BRIEF SUMMARY OF THE ROSARY'S HISTORY

Below is a very brief summary of the Rosary's history. If you want a somewhat more detailed look at what might be the Rosary's missing history, skip to the next section.

Here's the summary:

•••••••••

Church tradition credits St. Dominic, founder of the Dominicans, with the origins of today's Rosary. St. Dominic lived in the 12th and 13th centuries. However, there doesn't appear to be substantive evidence that the Rosary came from him at all, at least as far as we can know today. Many popes, who are not necessarily historians, have also credited St. Dominic with its origin. Yet, no biographies of St. Dominic during or soon after his time reportedly even mention an appearance of Our Lady to St. Dominic to give him the Rosary.

Over two hundred years later, another Dominican, Alan de la Roche, reported having a vision of St. Dominic with the story of Our Lady's appearance to him. That appears to be where the tradition of today began.

Not only is there no evidence that the Rosary of today can be traced back to St. Dominic, there is also no evidence that the Rosary's first sets of mysteries, as we know them today, can be traced back to him. There is a different Dominic from whom some meditations may have come, although not the recognizable three or four traditional sets of mysteries that we pray today.

Scholars on all sides of this debate have strong opinions about it. In the end, there is more to suggest that the Rosary we pray today did *not* originate from St. Dominic than that it did. In his time, it was not even called the Rosary.

The bottom line is that we don't have much concrete information about the history of today's Rosary. Its history seems to be missing.

Regardless of all this, as long as we acknowledge the significant problems with the Rosary's history, there are likely (mostly) good reasons to simply accept Church tradition and move on.

That's the summary. For a more comprehensive look at the Rosary's history, read the next section. Otherwise, skip past that section to *Going Beyond History* or to wherever you want to go.

# A LONGER HISTORY OF THE ROSARY

Although this section touches on many of the points of the Rosary's history, it's not complete. After all, this is not the main focus of this book. Nonetheless, you'll find many more details about its history in this section.

Most people in the Catholic Church, both clergy and lay, believe that the Rosary's history goes back to St. Dominic, the founder of the Dominican order. However, many serious scholars disagree with that. Often, they strongly disagree.

St. Dominic lived from 1170 to 1221 in the 12th and 13th centuries. He was canonized a saint on July 13, 1234, by Pope Gregory IX.

The lack of an agreed-upon history of the Rosary would come as a shock to most Catholics. Tradition in the Catholic Church has told us — for centuries — that the Rosary, as we think of it today, can be traced back to St. Dominic de Guzmán, the founder of the Dominicans. That tradition tells is understood to say that Our Lady appeared to St. Dominic to give him the Rosary.

But we find no existing evidence from his time documenting a vision of Our Lady to give St. Dominic the Rosary.

Over the centuries, many popes have supported that, crediting St. Dominic for the beginnings of what would become the Rosary of today.

Shouldn't these many popes know about that? Most popes are not historians, so not necessarily.

St. (Pope) John Paul II correctly said that the Rosary *"... gradually took form in the second millennium under the guidance of the Spirit of God."*[5]

It was actually over two hundred years after St. Dominic that the Dominican, Alan de la Roche (1428-1475), reported a vision revealing to him the appearance of Our Lady to St. Dominic during which she gave him the Rosary. Alan de la

---

[5] *This is from the beginning of the* Apostolic Letter, Rosarium Virginis Mariae Of The Supreme Pontiff John Paul II To The Bishops, Clergy And Faithful On The Most Holy Rosary, *October 16, 2002.*

Roche appears today to be the original source of the vision to St. Dominic as it has been traditionally believed.[6]

Some writers point to what they feel are unusual aspects of Alan de la Roche which they feel might throw doubt on his reported vision. Others don't see those things at all. Instead, they point to the "sanctity and scholarly character" of Alan de la Roche. Nonetheless, Alan de la Roche is credited by most with restoring the Rosary in his time.

The history of rosary-type prayer beads goes back hundreds of years before the time of St. Dominic. Historically, they have also been used outside of Christianity, though in different forms for different prayer purposes. However, here we only talk about the specific origins of the Rosary that we know and pray today.

Regarding all this, in *The Rose-Garden Game* (1969), Eithne Wilkins wrote:

> *"Historians, including Dominicans, point out that there is no evidence that St. Dominic himself had anything to do with inventing or developing the Rosary. On the other hand, a series of popes have officially approved the tradition that he had [invented or developed the Rosary], and the Dominican order is, as it were, in charge of the Rosary."* [Capitalization adjusted for clarity.]

St. Dominic was a remarkable saint. He had nothing at all to do with this confusion. As far as we can know today, he never personally claimed that Our Lady appeared to him to give him the Rosary during his lifetime. Those who knew St. Dominic and who wrote about him soon after his death never mentioned it. So let none of this reflect poorly on the great St. Dominic around whose life this controversy swirls.

One would understandably ask, however, why no one in St. Dominic's time knew that such an apparition happened.

---

[6] *Alan de la Roche is also known as Alain de la Roche, Alanus de Rupibus, and Alanus do Rupe. In some books, especially older ones, he is called "Blessed." However, it does not appear that he was ever officially beatified by the Catholic Church.*

Wouldn't almost everyone have known about such a significant happening in the life of this saint as the appearance of Our Lady? Was there really no mention of it in his biographies at the time? Did he not tell anyone? What makes Catholic tradition so sure that Our Lady gave the Rosary to St. Dominic when no one at the time appeared to know anything about it?

For a long time, even artists never added a rosary or a representation of a vision from Our Lady to their works of St. Dominic. Was Dominic really involved in the Rosary's history at all? The cards of currently-known history appear stacked against it.

I remain open to uncovering new evidence that might address these legitimate concerns. But there seems to be no available evidence that the origins of the Rosary we pray today began with St. Dominic. That includes the mysteries. That includes the name "Rosary."

According to Eithne Wilkins, it was not until the year 1475, under Pope Sixtus IV, that the "Marian Psalter" (sometimes called the Angelic Psalter) finally became known as the Rosary.[7] St. Dominic died in 1221, well over 250 years before the name of the devotion became known as the "Rosary."[8]

A different Dominic — Dominic of Prussia (1382-1461, sometimes given as different years) — is credited with attaching meditations to the Hail Marys. (Perhaps Alan de la Roche confused his Dominics.)

The Rosary of this second Dominic was still called the "Psalter of Mary," as it was also known in earlier times. Dominic of Prussia developed meditations for the 150 Hail

---

[7] *The controversial Pope Sixtus IV also established the feast of the Immaculate Conception on December 8th for the western Church.*

[8] *In* The History of St. Dominic *by Augusta Theodosia Drane, there is reference to a document, a last will and testament, of Anthony Sets who, in 1221, the year of St. Dominic's death, notes that he was a member of the Confraternity of the Holy Rosary. If valid and credible — and the author has not confirmed it and holds some skepticism — that would certainly give credibility to the existence of the term "Rosary" in the time of St. Dominic. However, also note a coming footnote of a Dominican scholar disputing the scholarship of Augusta Drane as a historian.*

Marys from the lives of Jesus and Mary. (Hail Marys were also shorter in his time.) Although some meditations have come down to us as part of the current mysteries, there is doubt that he can be fully credited with developing the original three sets of mysteries: Joyful, Sorrowful, and Glorious.

In light of all this, it is likely that, today, full and credible evidence of the Rosary's true history, especially back to St. Dominic of the Dominicans, does not exist.

On the other side of this, a reasoned case for accepting tradition, and a defense of Alan de la Roche, is made by Dominican Father Paul A. Duffner, O.P. in his article entitled, *The Rosary & St. Dominic • In Defense of A Tradition,* which first appeared in *The Rosary Light & Life* – Vol 49, No 5, September-October 1996.[9] Other writers have also supported Alan de la Roche's account over the years.

Note that "O.P." after the name of priests and other Dominicans stands for Order of Preachers. It is the more formal name for Dominicans.

Father Duffner suggests that actual evidence supporting St. Dominic and the Rosary, along with numerous other documents, may have once existed only to be destroyed by fire years after St. Dominic's time.

However, even had a later fire not destroyed many books and documents, it is still difficult to explain the total absence of any mentions of this story in art or in the early surviving biographies of St. Dominic.

As mentioned, many scholars have strong feelings on both sides of the Rosary's history. Yet, despite strong arguments against tying it to St. Dominic, that history remains firmly entrenched in the tradition of the Catholic Church.

*The History of St. Dominic* by Augusta Theodosia Drane (1891) contains a discussion of the Rosary's debated history in Chapter X: St Dominic and The Holy Rosary. Two sentences from that chapter stand out to the author concerning its history:

---

[9] *If still available, find the article at rosarycenter.org, accessed and available as of 10-11-2021.*

*To use the words of one who has devoted extraordinary care and diligence to the critical examination of the whole subject, "The Rosary has no history and will probably never have one."* (That last quote is credited to Fr. Père Antoine Danzas.)[10]

Augusta Drane continued:

*Like so many other of the more exquisite of God's gifts to men, like the life of her by whose virginal hands it was bestowed, the early history of this devotion is shrouded in silence and reserve.*

Nonetheless, although critical of early biographies of the saint and after presenting a case for skepticism of St. Dominic as the Rosary's origin — calling it a "legend" — even Augusta Drane feels that there is adequate reason to accept the tradition of today's Rosary tracing back to St. Dominic. She concludes by writing:

*"Rome has spoken, the cause is decided, and in presence of the authoritative decisions of [a long line] of august Pontiffs ... criticism must henceforth be put to silence."*

Based on other interpretations of the facts of history, many scholars strongly disagree with Augusta Drane's conclusion in her acceptance of Church tradition.

Regardless, if there is ever to be a resolution — and there may never be one — there is something to be said for her path.

A strong defense of St. Dominic's role in the Rosary is also made in an online writing by Dominican Romeo Maria del Santo Niño, O.P. That writing includes this:

*Because many documents have now been lost, it will not*

---

[10] *Here is Augusta Drane's comment and full citation for this quote, as cited by Augusta Drane:* "Fr. Père Antoine Danzas, in the exhaustive chapter on the Rosary which is to be found in the fourth volume of his Etudes sur les temps primitifs de l' Ordre de St. Dominique."

*be easy to prove historically that the Rosary originated from Saint Dominic. However, although the belief is not easy to prove historically, it is possible to show why it is reasonable and justified to hold the traditional belief. The reason is because, against the skepticism of the critics is a strong Papal tradition pointing to Saint Dominic as the author of the Rosary.*[11]
[Capitalization adjusted for consistency.]

There is much more in Dominic's defense on that website. In an answer to a question wondering whether St. Dominic received the Rosary from Our Lady, the author (Romeo Maria del Santo Niño) responded:

*Personally I believe that the Blessed Virgin did give the Rosary to St. Dominic, as described in the apparitions cited in the blog above* [its website is noted in the footnote above]. *However, the Rosary that the Blessed Virgin gave to St. Dominic was the primitive form of the Marian Psalter, not the form of the Rosary as it exists today. During the time of St. Dominic they prayed only the first half of the Hail Mary, and there were only 150 Hail Marys in the Rosary, which matched the 150 psalms of King David. Also, although meditation on the joyful, sorrowful and glorious events in the life of our Lord accompanied the prayer, the 15 mysteries were not fully defined yet.*

Recall that it was likely the second Dominic — Dominic of Prussia — from whom the mysteries can likely be traced, though not the separated and finished mysteries today.

•••••••••

A complete review of the complex history of the St. Dominic Rosary story is beyond this book's space and intent. Anyone searching for that full history using just a couple of sources will almost assuredly be left with incomplete, even erroneous

---

[11] *If it remains available, find the full writing at: thetheologycorner.com/the-origin-of-the-rosary, accessed 12-12-2021.*

information. In addition, certain books and documents that might provide additional research help aren't readily available anymore.

However, interested readers are welcome to start down the complicated road to understanding the Rosary's full history — the Rosary as we know it today. Don't expect an easy journey.

Today, it may be fair to say, as Augusta Drane relays to us from Père Danzas, *"The Rosary has no history and will probably never have one."* Of course, there clearly has to be an accurate history of today's Rosary somewhere. It just seems to be missing.[12]

St. John Paul II reminded us that *"The Rosary is by its nature a prayer for peace."* Indeed, it is often used to pray for peace, while also being credited with winning battles. It would be good if we could stop being concerned about its complex history so as to bring some peace to ourselves. In the long run, its history may not even matter, other than as an academic exercise that may never reach a satisfactory conclusion.

Regardless of what has been said above, it's likely beneficial for both peace and unity — and possibly even for a yet-to-be-uncovered reality — that we accept the tradition of the Church as best as we can and move on.

However, should one insist on using the "traditional" history for some modern argumentative purpose, then we would indeed be justified to look critically at its origins.

Nonetheless, when, with others, popes of the stature of Pope Leo XIII expressly affirmed that the Rosary was entrusted to St. Dominic from Our Lady, neither can we easily ignore their insights.

It is certainly understandable that one asks with confusion, *"What actually is the Rosary's history?"* — but then receives no historically definitive answer.

---

[12] *If you are a daring researcher, you might want to start with The Rose-Garden Game (1969) by Eithne Wilkins. Chapter One offers a strong argument against the tradition of St. Dominic and the rosary. Of course, there are also many other sources. Sadly, you'll find a number of other authors don't seem to have adequately researched the question themselves. So be cautious—and good luck to you!*

To the potentially more straightforward question, *What is the Rosary?*, a little prayerbook's response, from 1888, likely represents the majority of responses over hundreds of years, including through today, when its author wrote:

> *"It is an easy and simple form of oral and mental prayer, introduced by St. Dominic in the thirteenth century, heartily approved by the Church, and to this day recommended and practiced fervently."* [*Catholic Worship: The Sacraments, Ceremonies, and Festivals of the Church* by Rev. O. Gisler.]

In what should be the bottom line, when Our Lady has spoken to us in multiple apparitions, she has never been concerned about whether or not the full and correct history of her Rosary is known to us.

She just wants us to pray it.

## GOING BEYOND HISTORY

The Rosary is a contemplative prayer. But it is not a single prayer: it's a *framework* of prayer. Within its framework, multiple prayers and meditations take place. As we pray the Rosary, we meditate on moments from Scripture as we examine our own lives and spirituality. We can recognize our shortcomings and determine to become better people in the eyes of both God and man (generically speaking). Prayed correctly, the Rosary brings us closer to faith, as well as to a greater love of God.

*"The cycles of meditation proposed by the Holy Rosary are by no means exhaustive, but they do bring to mind what is essential and they awaken in the soul a thirst for a knowledge of Christ continually nourished by the pure source of the Gospel* [St. John Paul II].*"*

On October 16, 2002, when as pope, Saint John Paul II presented the Luminous Mysteries, some people refused to accept them. There is no evidence they were from Our Lady and, so their thinking sometimes goes, no one should add to or change the Rosary they grew up with and that they recited throughout their lives — unless Our Lady comes down to personally tell them that it's okay to add or change something. Of course, these new mysteries are not required anymore than the Rosary itself is required — and it's not.

One can go online today and find the Rosary prayed beautifully in some daily videos — but without the Luminous Mysteries.

While saying there is "nothing wrong" with the Luminous Mysteries, one online writer nonetheless almost appeared to demean them, calling them "not traditional." The writer said to pray the 15 decades of the original "traditional" mysteries — leaving out the Luminous Mysteries. This clergyman, then credited St. Dominic both with the Rosary itself as well as, apparently, with giving us the Joyful, Sorrowful, and Glorious mysteries. We already know it is improbable that either of those things actually came from St. Dominic, especially the specific mysteries as we know them today.

The Luminous Mysteries are wonderful and appropriate. St. John Paul II gave them to us. To ignore them is a loss to everyone who chooses not to say and meditate upon them.

But wait! Why would some people choose to disregard the Luminous Mysteries because they came from a pope (now a great saint) — but not from St. Dominic — while accepting the new mysteries of Pope Clement XIV in the 1700s, who reportedly replaced the last two Glorious Mysteries?

Replaced the last two Glorious Mysteries, you ask? According to a preeminent historical scholar and Dominican priest,[13] the original 4th and 5th Glorious Mysteries were:

(4) The Second Coming, and (5) The General Judgment.

Pope Clement XIV — pope from 1769–1774 — appears to have changed them to the two Marian mysteries of today:

(4) The Assumption, and (5) The Crowning of Our Lady as Queen of Heaven and Earth.

So which two Glorious Mysteries are the "traditional" mysteries, those before or those after Pope Clement XIV?

And if wanting some ill-defined "traditional" Rosary, why would some traditionalists not go back to one of the earlier forms of the Hail Mary, including the absence of its last sentence and even the name Jesus? Indeed, why not go back to saying the Latin form of that shorter prayer? Where is the line drawn where so-called "traditionalists" might stop complaining and accept what is widely accepted and prayed today? Even Fatima does not define the parameters of a Rosary that will never change. The Rosary has changed and will likely continue to do so.

The bottom line is that people who don't want change can't go back far enough to a time before change.

We all connect with others in the worldwide Church in

---

[13] *In an email to the author of September 25, 2021, Father Augustine Thompson O.P., Professor of History, Dominican School of Philosophy and Theology, felt that Pope Clement XIV's change to the Marian mysteries was unfortunate. Additionally, Father Thompson suggested that Augusta Drane was not a competent historian. The author is grateful for Father Thompson's assistance identifying two (other) important sources for this project. [Disclaimer: Father Thompson has not viewed, reviewed, approved, or been involved in any way in the production of this book.]*

accepting past, current, and coming changes to both the Rosary and the Church itself.

•••••••••

There are always those in the Catholic Church (really in any church) who are unwilling to change. They feel the Church should stay "as it's always been." Somehow, they feel that the Church must be violating some long-held Jesus-approved prayers, liturgies, or teachings. They do not understand that the Church has never "always been" the same, even at its beginning.

Separately from the core teachings of the Church which, while periodically being clarified for the faithful have been consistent, change has been a constant. Significantly greater changes, even in basic teachings, have been seen throughout the history of many other churches.

The teachings of Jesus have been consistent, as have foundational linkages to His teachings in faith and morals. But things surrounding much else have changed over the centuries — and they continue to change.

When people complain, they aren't really saying that they want the Church to be what it used to be — although that's what they think they're saying.

They're actually saying that they want the Church to be the same as *when they were growing up.* They want the memories, prayers, and worship of their childhood — that then stretched into their adulthood — to stay the same. They don't want the Church to change the warm feelings they have always had for things in the Church.

Rarely, if ever, do those people actually want the Church to go back to "how it used to be" — to how it was after Jesus died and during the earliest times of the apostolic mission work. They don't even want the Church to go back to the second or third centuries. They want it to go back to a much later time — to what they remember, what they liked, and how it was when they grew up. They want the Catholic Church to be a comfortable *unchanging* home for them.

The Church *is* home. But it has always changed. Sometimes we like the changes. Other times, changes can be less comfortable and harder to get used to. Sometimes we *really* don't like certain changes. But Scripture is clear that Jesus said He would always be with the Church which He founded as He sent His apostles into the world. That was the beginning of what is the Catholic Church. *"And behold, I am with you always, to the end of the world."* [Matthew 28:20.]

Too many people forget that or they twist the words of Jesus so that they can wrongly say that He meant something different. Some want to believe that, regardless of its clear history, Jesus meant some different church.

However, early history combined with earliest Christian writings clearly support only one original Christian church: the Catholic Church. In spite of ups and downs, evidence of its strength in the world has remained. It has always been the largest and most preeminent Christian church in the world.

Those forgetting this history don't just include Catholics. They include all those who broke from Catholicism after the Protestant Reformation — and the countless Reformation-descendant churches that have multiplied into being today.

Whether in its clergy or laity, the Roman Catholic Church is a church of imperfect people doing what we can, imperfectly, to get to heaven. Therefore, we must be patient with each other — and with the Church itself.

Jesus came down to bring change. But He never said that things shouldn't change after He was gone. He put Peter in charge of His young church [Matthew 16:18]. Jesus knew that decisions would have to be made in the future. Perhaps He might have hoped that changes would be good and carefully done. But He *is* God. He would have also known that things wouldn't be perfect. At times, things would be *very* imperfect.

We can look back at the history of the Church in the Middle Ages — and at other times — to see many examples of such imperfection. That has almost always been caused by imperfect people of which, remember, the Church is composed. Yet, in spite of internal and external problems over many centuries, the teachings of Jesus have remained firm and constant in the Catholic Church.

•••••••••

We see in the history of the Rosary that it has never existed in a single form, with today's structure and prayers, as many people assume. Even accepting Alan de la Roche's report that Mary gave the Rosary to St. Dominic, Mary would not have come down to hand St. Dominic an inviolate book on how to say the Rosary, with all its current mysteries, prayers, and everything that we do today spelled out in it. Instead, the Rosary has evolved. Over the centuries, it has become a stronger and stronger prayer.

Although it is good to stay close to its more broadly shared structure when we pray the Rosary today (subject to continuing change, of course), nonetheless it is flexible enough to use in the direction which our personal spirituality and prayer lead us.

Changes to the Rosary continued both at Fatima and after the time of Fatima. Today, it is an especially powerful and beautiful prayer. As we already heard, the Hail Mary itself used to be a much shorter prayer. It has gone through several changes over the centuries.

At her apparitions at Fatima in 1917, Our Lady strongly encouraged praying the Rosary. Indeed, she called herself *"Our Lady of The Rosary."* It is from those apparitions that the Fatima Prayer came, now almost always said at the end of each decade of the Rosary. That prayer became yet another change, another addition to the Rosary.

The totality of evidence confirming Our Lady's apparitions at Fatima is overwhelming. Those questioning those apparitions either haven't seen the entirety of that evidence — or they simply refuse to accept evidence of any sort, no matter what it might be.

We also find the Rosary in the famed apparitions of Our Lady to St. Bernadette at Lourdes, France, in 1858, as well as in other apparitions. Those include her 1973 apparitions to the visionary, Sister Agnes, at Akita, Japan. During those apparitions, serious admonitions were given. There Our Lady, again, strongly encouraged praying the Rosary daily. (Sister Agnes died on August 15, 2024 — the Feast of the Assumption of Our Lady.)

It was Pope Leo XIII (1810—1903; pope from 1878 to 1903) who on December 10, 1883 added Our Lady's title as Queen of the Rosary to the Litany of the Blessed Virgin. Pope Leo encouraged the faithful to pray the Rosary devotion everyday.[14] Note that it was from this pope that the prayer to St. Michael (the Archangel) came on October 13, 1884.

Pope Leo XIII's Encyclical given on September 1, 1883, related to the Rosary, along with related letters of the Pope, were said *"to constitute a new epoch in the history of this devotion."*[15]

In an article titled, *Leo XIII and the Rosary*, appearing in the May 2003 issue of the respected *homiletic & pastoral review*, the Reverend James Buckley, F.S.S.P., wrote:

> *"No successor of St. Peter, however, promoted this devotion [the Rosary] as continually as Pope Leo XIII. During his twenty-five year reign, this saintly pope wrote no fewer that 11 encyclicals extolling the devotion and strenuously encouraging the faithful to practice it."*

Not listed here are several interesting parallels between Pope Leo XIII and Pope John Paul II, both of whom are considered special popes of Our Lady. Pope John Paul II has been called the Pope of Fatima.[16]

The Rosary has evolved over centuries. In relatively recent

---

[14] *This is as per* The Excellence of the Rosary *(1912) by Reverend M.J. Frings (reprinted by Refuge of Sinners Publishing in 2019). The future Pope Leo XIII was born one day after the birth of the great pianist and composer, Frédérick Chopin. The pope at that time, Pope Pius VII, had been wrongly imprisoned at the time the future Pope Leo XIII was born. (Going forward a bit over a century, Pope John Paul II was born two days after Joan of Arc was canonized by Pope Benedict XV. Born under Pope Benedict XV, Pope John Paul II would be succeeded as pope by Pope Benedict XVI.) Leo XIII's predecessor as pope was Blessed (Pope) Pius IX who, among other things, declared Our Lady's Immaculate Conception as dogma, called the First Vatican Council, and has been the longest serving pope (1846 - 1878).*

[15] *As per the Translator's Preface (by Rev. Stephen Byrne, O.P.) to* Meditations on the Mysteries of the Holy Rosary *(1885) by Father Monsabre, O.P., reprinted by Refuge of Sinners Publishing in 2019.*

[16] *See, for example,* His Angels at Our Side: Understanding Their Power in Our Souls and the World *by Fr. John Horgan (2018; EWTN Publishing).*

times, it seems to be changing at an even faster rate, primarily — as has been the case over hundreds of years — as new things are added. The changes all seem to have strengthened the Rosary, and the development of our spirituality, as we pray it.

In its short section on *How To Say The Rosary,* a little book from 1932 tells us that the opening prayers of the Rosary — the Apostle's Creed, Our Father, three Hail Marys — are *"not an essential part of the Rosary."*[17] That may have been true in the past, but one would be hard-pressed to find people praying the Rosary today who say that they skip those prayers when beginning a Rosary. All appear to believe that they are an integral part of the Rosary.

Although the things presented in the book currently in your hands, or to which you are now listening, are not yet firmly established in the same way as other elements of the Rosary, the elements here are consistent with its historical and spiritual progression.

Regardless of past changes and additions to the Rosary, concerns about the Rosary's history (or about continuing changes over the years) should recede to the background in favor of praying the Rosary itself. Its use should benefit whatever personal spiritual growth and benefits each of us can gain from it. Its use should bring us closer to God and to Our Lady — even to each other.

In the end, a study of the Rosary's history isn't what's important. Praying it daily is.

---

[17] *As per* Ave Maria: Thoughts on the Mysteries of the Holy Rosary, *by Rev. J.E. Moffatt, S.J., 1932.*

# IS THE ROSARY UNSCRIPTURAL?

Non-Catholics, especially Evangelicals and other protestant sects, believe that saying the Rosary is a vain and mindless repetition of prayer. After all, some logically say, without at least some attention to prayer, is prayer even prayer at all? But does that mean that every single prayer must be sincere and from the heart? Or is imperfect prayer better than no prayer at all? What *is* prayer? Some of the fiercest anti-Catholic critics believe that they know — and they believe that it's not what Catholics do.

Critics attacking the Rosary say that Scripture teaches against repetition of prayer, as is clearly done when praying the Rosary. They extend their logic insisting that Catholicism violates Scripture. They claim that the Rosary is just one example of that. Some go further, condemning the entirety of the Catholic Church as not being scriptural. They are totally wrong in their belief. They don't understand the intimate, historical involvement of the Catholic Church with Scripture.

Many non-Catholics also attack the close connection to Mary that Catholics have. They are wrong there, too. But this is not the place to address every incorrect understanding of Catholicism — and there are a number of them. Here, I just talk about the Rosary.

To support their criticism of repetition of prayers, non-Catholic Christians often point to Matthew 6:7 as support. Perhaps unknowingly, some must twist the context and words of Scripture in order to do that.

We read this in Matthew 6:7:

*"When you pray, do not go on babbling endlessly as the pagans do, for they believe that they are more likely to be heard because of their many words."* (NCB)

However, the King James version translates that same verse as:

*"But when ye pray, use not <u>vain repetitions</u>, as the heathen do: for they think that they shall be heard for their much speaking."* [KJV: *Emphasis added.*]

31

Many non-Catholics still use the King James version of the Bible. That's why they refer to "vain repetitions" in their criticism, not just of the Rosary, but of other formulaic prayers. Some of those prayers are certainly among the most beautiful (consider the Memorare as one example).

The Rosary is certainly not "babbling," nor are those who pray it *correctly* involved with any "vain repetitions." Matthew 6:7 does caution against those who try to show off with a false piety in front of others, trying to demonstrate how spiritual they think they are. But that's not the only time Scripture cautions against insincere prayers.

In Mark 12:38–40, we read this:

> *"Beware of the scribes, who like to walk around in long robes, to be greeted respectfully in the marketplace, and to have the best seats in the synagogues and the places of honor at banquets. They devour the houses of widows, while for the sake of appearance they recite lengthy prayers. They will receive the severest possible condemnation."* [Emphasis added.]

It's not repetition that is the problem. It's the absence of prayerful spirituality, humility, caring, and sincere attention to one's prayers that is the problem — whether Catholic or non-Catholic. The problem is with the absence of those things which make prayer, prayer.

Jesus was clear whom He was condemning and why. It doesn't matter whether or not the scribes repeated their prayers or not. What mattered was that their prayers were insincere, done *"for the sake of appearance."* That's not praying.

One does not have to repeat a prayer to pray without faith or sincerity. That can happen to those who do not practice spiritual discipline in any prayer, regardless of repetition.

One way to help us develop such discipline, as we will see shortly, is to pray *more*.

As was just said, the Rosary is not a mindless repetition of prayers — unless people wrongly use it that way. Prayed correctly, the Rosary is an amazingly rich and complex prayer. It does not violate Scripture at all. Instead, it is consistent with Scripture and with the scriptural tasking to pray without ceasing.

In the book, *The Life of Saint Dominic* by Bede Jarrett, O.P., we find this:

*For, after all, the very repetition of words... deadens the senses to the world about and opens the understanding of the soul to other and higher plains of thought.*

So, properly done, repetition can help to clear the mind so that we can focus on the things of God. In the case of the Rosary, that focus is often in meditating on the mysteries of the Rosary. Nonetheless, we can also enjoy the simple rhythm and peace of the Rosary prayers.

As one prays more, there is an increase in contemplation on the things of God as well as on our own need for spiritual strength and growth.

This is not to say that the individual prayers of the Rosary are not important and beneficial in themselves. They are. But they are just one element of the Rosary.

Reflecting on the Hail Mary in his book, The *True Devotion to the Blessed Virgin*,[18] the beloved Saint Louis Marie Grignion de Montfort (1673-1716) wrote:[19]

*"When the Hail Mary is well said, that is, with attention, devotion and humility, it is, according to the saints, the enemy of Satan, putting him to flight; it is the hammer that crushes him, a source of holiness for souls, a joy to the angels and a sweet melody for the devout."*

Therefore, the Rosary is more than just saying "a bunch of Hail Marys." People can certainly concentrate on each Hail Mary, though even the most spiritually disciplined can sometimes find their minds drifting. However, the individual

---

[18] *Originally known as* A Treatise on the True Devotion to the Blessed Virgin by the Venerable Servant of God, *this famous book was written in French in 1712.*

[19] *Louis De Montfort was canonized by Pope Pius XII in 1947. His biography is recommended.*

prayers are just a part of the total prayerfulness of the Rosary.

More significant are the meditations on the various mysteries that accompany each decade. Those meditations should extend further as we meditate on how the lessons of each mystery impact our lives — and how our lives should change to become closer to God. These are what make the Rosary anything but a simple and mindless activity. Sincere prayer from the heart defines a well-said Rosary.

But importantly, we add this:

> *"This form of prayerful reflection* [meditating on the mysteries of Christ] *is of great value, but Christian prayer should go further: to the knowledge of the love of the Lord Jesus, to union with him."* [Catechism of the Catholic Church, 2nd Edition, §2708.]

In his wonderful Apostolic Letter on the Rosary — recommended to the reader — then Pope, now Saint John Paul II wrote:

> *"Without contemplation, the Rosary is a body without a soul, and its recitation runs the risk of becoming a mechanical repetition of formulas, in violation of the admonition of Christ: 'In praying do not heap up empty phrases as the Gentiles do; for they think they will be heard for their many words' (Mt 6:7). By its nature the recitation of the Rosary calls for a quiet rhythm and a lingering pace, helping the individual to meditate on the mysteries of the Lord's life as seen through the eyes of her who was closest to the Lord. In this way the unfathomable riches of these mysteries are disclosed."*[20]

Of course, people can "babble" any prayer. People can certainly repeat prayers, by rote, without thinking about what they're saying *and* without meditating on spiritual or biblical mysteries. All of our minds can drift at times if we can't

---

[20] *From the previously quoted Chapter One (12) of the* Apostolic Letter, Rosarium Virginis Mariae Of The Supreme Pontiff John Paul II, *October 16, 2002.*

establish ongoing self-discipline in prayer. Minds can drift in prayer even if we're not repeating anything.

Spiritual discipline in prayer takes work. Later, we'll look at Meditation Beads, a small tool to provide a little help for those whose minds drift (as most of ours do, at times) while praying the Rosary.

As with anything else, we must learn how to use and pray the Rosary, vocally aloud when possible and not disruptive to others. It's not hard, but it's not intuitive for everyone. People should not feel compelled to pray vocally if a higher level of prayer is strong within us.

Although the Rosary is often encouraged as vocal prayer, it's not easy for some to consistently meditate on the mysteries while saying the prayers aloud. For many, it's easier to say the Rosary prayers quietly or in silence while becoming more disciplined meditating on the mysteries. Be flexible. But pray regularly. Good prayer is a habit.

It's also simple to meditate on the mystery — being sure not to rush the meditation — before starting the decade, and also at the Meditation Bead when one is available (see Chapter Three). After the meditation, one can then concentrate on the individual prayers while saying them either aloud or quietly. But, whether aloud or in silence, be sincere in prayer. Pray from the heart.

Fortunately, the more we pray the Rosary, the better it gets — and the richer becomes our connection to God.

More generally, we must simply learn to pray.

At Medjugorje, Our Lady told us something very insightful. She said that we should *"Pray until prayer becomes a joy for you."*

Why are those such perceptive words? Because they assume that prayer is *not* necessarily a joy for us. Indeed, it can be drudgery for some. Our Lady clearly knows that.

What's Our Lady's answer to prayer that isn't "a joy" yet?

*Pray more!*

How much more?

*"Pray until prayer becomes a joy for you."*

The more we pray *from the heart,* the easier and more meaningful prayer becomes. At last — and it can take a while — it *does* become a joy for us. It's what Our Lady said, and, done correctly, it's what happens.

So pray more, especially using the Rosary. It is a powerful and flexible way to pray.

•••••••••

But why do many non-Catholics continue to berate Catholics and the Rosary, condemning it as "vain repetition" of prayer?

Astoundingly, some protestants have even been taught not to say the *Our Father* too often lest it, too, become "vain repetition."

But wait! That's the prayer Jesus told us to pray! He was asked how to pray, and that's what He taught us!

Would Jesus have meant that we should just say it one time, total? Or maybe no more than just once a day?

Of course, not. If that had been a concern for Jesus, He would have told us. He knows human frailty.

At least one non-Catholic called the Our Father simply a "teaching tool." It's seemingly something to be used as a prayer *starter* for beginners before moving on to what that person seemed to feel is more important praying.[21]

That's absurd. It's the prayer that Jesus Himself gave us. For countless centuries it has been the core prayer for Christians.

One writer actually said he had once been taught that *"The Lord's prayer wasn't really to be prayed verbatim because that was 'vain repetition' and Jesus said not to do that."*[22]

Although those examples might seem extreme (they are), they illustrate the real misunderstandings too many have about Catholics and prayer. They are an example of the scriptural confusion of many non-Catholic Christians.

Then there are the many anti-Catholics who refuse to do things just because Catholics do them. If it's a Catholic prayer, practice, or teaching, many anti-Catholics refuse to accept it, no matter how scriptural, beneficial, or effective such things

---

[21] *If still available, see this comment following this article: https:// mattdabbs.com/2017/11/20/not-all-repetition-is-vain-repetition-developing-a-more-vibrant-prayer-life, accessed 8-30-2021.*

[22] *See: https://mattdabbs.com/2017/11/20/not-all-repetition-is-vain-repetition-developing-a-more-vibrant-prayer-life, accessed 8-30-2021.*

might be.

Remember the parable of the persistent widow in Luke 18:1-8? She waited and waited for a judge to rule in her case. The judge didn't care. He just kept putting her off. But the widow persisted. She bothered the judge so often with her request to rule in her case that he finally gave in.

As the widow persisted without becoming weary, so we, too, must *"pray always and never... lose heart."* [Luke 18:1.] She believed that she could secure a just verdict from the judge and repeatedly insisted on it. Her belief eventually got her that just verdict. She had faith. We, too, must have faith in prayer. If we don't, *"...when the Son of Man comes, will He find faith on the earth?"* [Luke 18:8.]

Among other things, she is an example of persistence. Did the widow ensure that she didn't repeat herself each time she spoke to the judge? Of course not. She said the same things and made the same request each time. Finally, she got what she asked for. She knew that she would. She had faith in herself and in her many requests.

Also, consider Luke 11:5-9. In a parable, Jesus told us that if we don't get something that we ask for (assuming it's a good and proper request), we should be persistent. Effectively that means we should continue to submit our request over and over. Be patient. Be persistent. Don't give up.

On February 22, 1931, Jesus appeared in a special way to Sister, now Saint, Faustina (1905-1938), and spoke to her. Not only did He not caution against repetition, we were given another prayer full of repetition: the Chaplet of the Divine Mercy.

It seems that there is power in repetition. It's how we memorize things. It's how we learn in general. It's how children get what they want from their parents. Lyrics in songs are commonly repeated. Are not the words of lovers to each other repetitious?

Those who insist that there should be no repetition in prayer are actively discouraging prayer. For those who wrongly follow that advice, prayers are reduced in both frequency and quality.

Whose interests are served by people whose advice can only discourage sincere prayer?

Not God's.

# NO TIME FOR GOD?

Data in many countries continue to show an increasing number of people who no longer consider themselves part of any traditional church. Some complain, *"I don't need some so-called 'church' telling me what to believe! I have God in my heart! I can just talk to Him directly — if I want. That's enough!"*

Certainly, we can and should talk directly to God. But is it true that it is enough?

It doesn't take a theologian to know that it's generally not enough. On January 9, 2022, Joe Namath observed, *"You learn you don't do much on your own...in this life. We need help. We need to carry respect with us, and love our neighbors..."*[23]

There was a reason that the disciples of Jesus were together, as a believing community, supporting each other. They weren't just a bunch of individuals doing their own thing by themselves.

In reality, many people no longer seriously believe, or even care, that God exists — including many who tell others, or themselves, that they believe in God.

Can people today give any logical arguments for the existence of God? Most can't. They themselves may have a strong faith that God exists, but they can't give a non-believer good reasons to understand that God exists.

Many years ago, people could do that. The classic, foundational book, the *Summa Theologica,* written by St. Thomas Aquinas in the 13th century, lays out several arguments for the existence of God. Today, few know what they are.

•••••••••

The devil is not merely a child's nightmare or fantasy. Evil exists. And it is Satan's work to keep us away from God.

---

[23] *Joe Namath was one of American football's greatest players and representatives.*

How can Satan succeed in his task of taking souls away from God? To win, Satan doesn't necessarily have to lead people into sin as people think — although he does that. Satan just has to keep everyone so busy that we have no time for God, no time for prayer.

So far, and especially in the Western world, it's working. We see that sin is not the only thing that separates us from God.

Because our busyness doesn't seem like sin, people don't recognize the spiritual destruction that happens to us in our everyday lives. But, unless we turn back to God, especially through substantive daily prayer, we will not see God. Satan will have won.

Technology in itself isn't bad. It's exciting and it's helpful in our lives. But it's also addicting and time-consuming.

Check how many hours you're in front of a technology screen during the day. Some of that same technology can help you to keep track of that. It can let you know how much of your day is no longer available for God and prayer.

Technology (as we think of it today) takes our time over and above the time that we needed to live and work before today's technology existed. In pre-technology times, people had more time for God and for prayer, although they didn't always take advantage of it then either. Nonetheless, more time existed for God and prayer back then — if people chose to use it. There was more quiet time for ourselves, too.

Even though technology in itself isn't bad — it's clearly necessary today — the time it takes from us as it redirects us away from God *is* bad. But, even if we had none of today's technology, Satan would find something else for us to do, other ways to consume our time so that we have little or none left for God.

*An Aside: If faith in God alone were all that was necessary for salvation, would it even matter if we had no time for God and prayer? It would not. But faith alone is not enough. We need to be actively close to God in our daily lives. That closeness is most often achieved through prayer. But it also comes in doing those other things which Jesus and Scripture tell us that we must do. Why would Jesus tell us to do anything at all if only faith were needed? Faith is very important. But we are scripturally called to do more.*

It's not just technology that can take our time and separate us from God. There are many other things in our lives that can also do that. All this happens without our even knowing that it's happening.

So, indeed, it's not sin alone that can take us away from God and prayer.

Prayer, love, faith, and spiritual self-discipline are our weapons to fight back. But we're not using them often enough, if at all.

The war to take us away from God is a silent war — and we're losing the war. We need to consciously put on a new mantle of spirituality and fight back vigorously.

•••••••••

Even with time for regular prayer, we still have to be concerned about sin, about keeping God's commandments. We need to stop sinning. Today, we make excuses for committing sin — mostly sins of the flesh, but also others — telling ourselves that what used to be widely understood as sin really isn't anymore. That's real trouble for us.

Sure, along with other things, love and faith and prayer are important. But God, through Scripture, has repeatedly said that we must keep His commandments. Jesus has also said that in the Gospels.

For many, this component is ignored thinking that God will effectively love us into heaven. Sister Lucia, seer of Fatima, was very clear that that's not the case. We must also lead a life in conformity with God's commandments.

Do we even know what they are anymore?

Few do.

Knowing God's commandments goes well beyond a simple reading of the Ten Commandments.

This, too, is beyond the main focus of this book, but should be in our minds and lives regardless.

Our Lady at Medjugorje has often reminded us of this very thing. Note this admonition as part of her message of February 25, 2022: *"Little children, if you do not return to*

*God and His Commandments, you do not have a future."*

Given in the context of Russia's war on Ukraine, but with meaning that goes well beyond that, Our Lady's March 25, 2022 message from Medjugorje said, in part, *"I am calling you to return to God and to God's Commandments...that you may come out of this crisis into which you have entered because you are not listening to God who loves you..."*

# CHAPTER TWO

## The Loveful Mysteries

## THE LOVEFUL MYSTERIES
### Mysteries of Introspection
=========================
### Part One
=========================

Without love, we cannot share in the essence of God, because God *is* love.

As of this writing, the Loveful Mysteries are not part of the main canon of Rosary mysteries. However, although the structure of the Rosary and its prayers are widely accepted, shared, and prayed, things related to this powerful, flexible prayer, or to any prayer, are naturally at the discretion and needs of those who use it as part of their own sincere prayers.

Our Lady has been clear that we need to come back to God in both prayer and action. Our Lady has been telling us this for many years, for centuries.

*"We believe that we are saved ... through the grace of the Lord Jesus,"* [Acts 15:10]. However, Jesus's repeated teaching in Scripture is clear that, among other things, we must *also* keep God's commandments. So, even with grace and salvation through Jesus, our souls are still ours to save in obedience to the commandments if we want to be with God at the end of our journey.

On our journey, we should not underestimate the sacraments, teachings, wisdom, and graces found in the Catholic Church and the support of others who are on that same road.

••••••

What are the Loveful Mysteries? What purpose do they serve? Here are the mysteries with their related scriptural verses:

(1) No Greater Love [John 15:9-14];
(2) Whatever You Do For One (you do for Me)
    [Matthew 25:34-40; John 13:34-35];
(3) The Greatest Commandment [Matthew 22:36-40];
(4) The Beatitudes [Matthew 5:1-12];
(5) Pray Without Ceasing
    [1 Thessalonians 5:16-18; Mark 11:22-25].

The Loveful Mysteries share much in common with the other mysteries of the Rosary. However, two things stand out as different. Effectively all of the other mysteries (Joyful, Luminous, Sorrowful, Glorious) are reflections on events in the lives of Jesus and Mary. Those reflections not only allow us to consider those specific events, but also to look inside ourselves in light of those events.

The Loveful Mysteries also contain reflections based on Scripture. But their specialness appears to be, in part, in their significant interior reflections and meditations on our spiritual and daily lives — and how we can put those reflections into action. Of course, we should be doing that with the other mysteries, too.

The Loveful Mysteries are based on scriptural *teachings* more than on events.

As we think about the scriptural teachings on which the Loveful Mysteries rest, we can directly contemplate what we need to do to repair or strengthen our personal earthly and spiritual works in responding to the call of Jesus.

We'll start by looking at the Rosary, in general. Then we'll look at why the love within us — for God and for others — is so vital. Finally, we'll look at each Loveful Mystery in depth.

••••••

There are two basic kinds of Rosary prayer: public and private. Saying the Rosary in public is a shared experience among those praying. It links people in the power and commonality of familiar prayers.

Many people chime in to say that when two or three are gathered in Jesus's name, Jesus is in their midst (Matthew 18:20). But, when taken out of its broader context, that can be misleading.

For one thing, some might conclude that if two or three are NOT gathered together — if we pray by ourselves, for example — that Jesus is *not* with us. Do we rush out and find someone — anyone! — to pray with us so that Jesus will be with us? Of course, we don't. When we pray from the heart, Jesus can be with us, too.

Nonetheless, there is something powerful and unifying

when sharing a public Rosary with others. The public Rosary provides a shared commonality of beloved prayer. There has always been faith that, as we pray together, God is indeed in our midst, not just as we say the words, but especially when we pray from the heart.

In a public Rosary, the mystery is announced at the beginning of each decade. Although a leader will sometimes read a reflection on the mystery, there is rarely substantive time for meditation on each mystery.

That is because we generally concentrate on when it's our turn to say the prayer responses. We are more in tune with the mechanics, the rhythm, and the individual prayers of the Rosary than with the meditative depth that is possible when we pray alone. Of course, prayed from the heart, the Hail Marys and other Rosary prayers are important unto themselves.

In his Apostolic Letter of October 16, 2002, St. John Paul II wrote:

*In order to supply a Biblical foundation and greater depth to our meditation, it is helpful to follow the announcement of the mystery with the proclamation of a related Biblical passage, long or short, depending on the circumstances. No other words can ever match the efficacy of the inspired word. As we listen, we are certain that this is the word of God, spoken for today and spoken "for me."*[24]

Our Lady has asked that the Rosary be renewed and prayed in our families. When prayed carefully with supportive family members, family Rosaries can be a wonderful blend between a public and private Rosary.

*"We need to return to the practice of family prayer and prayer for families, continuing to use the Rosary* [St. John Paul II]*."*

---

[24] *From the previously quoted* Apostolic Letter, Rosarium Virginis Mariae Of The Supreme Pontiff John Paul II, *Chapter Three (30), October 16, 2002.*

In a strictly private Rosary, we not only announce (aloud or to ourselves) each mystery, we also meditate on that mystery throughout its decade. Meditating on the mysteries of the Rosary as we say the prayers, is foundational for praying the Rosary, especially when we are by ourselves.

Rosary Center.org says, *"While the lips are uttering the words of the Hail Marys, the mind dwells on the various mysteries. The ten Hail Marys function as a measuring device to determine the length of time to reflect on this event in the life of Jesus and His Mother."*

When alone, but certainly never when it is intrusive or irritating to others, it is certainly good to say the Rosary aloud. However, as mentioned before, meditation on the mysteries is the heart of the Rosary. If saying the Rosary aloud takes away too much from the meditations, say the Rosary quietly to yourself while meditating on the mysteries until you're better able to say it aloud while meditating.

But, aloud or to yourself, pray the Rosary.

There are many wonderful prayers in addition to the Rosary. Yet, in times of special spiritual danger or temptation, saying the Rosary, especially aloud, may provide special protection.

Don't just rush into the prayers of the Rosary. Before beginning, spend a bit of serious time considering your intention for the Rosary you are about to begin. Being specific here is better than just asking God for something in general terms. It is especially good to pray for some spiritual need, rather just for temporal goods. A good spiritual advisor can help us to develop a healthier prayer life.

Is it necessary to meditate on the mysteries every time you say the Rosary? Of course not. You can concentrate on the individual prayers. Don't always meditate on the mysteries so fully that the prayers are totally excluded.

However, the fullness of the Rosary is best when our focus is on the mysteries and how our own lives can be better in our reflections on them.

For many, the Hail Marys become akin to a background chant shielding those who pray from the world. If we are not attentive, the world can intrude on our prayers. We can easily be distracted from in-depth meditation on each mystery. As we heard earlier, Bede Jarrett, O.P., said, *"...the very repetition of words"* of the Rosary can protect us from the world while we pray.

Yet, regardless of our prayers, we are not always protected from the world. Our minds drift, frequently to thoughts that have no connection to the spiritual world at all. We often have to struggle to keep focused on the mysteries and on the things of God.

We overcome that with regular prayer by making a conscious effort to strengthen our spiritual and prayerful discipline. In the next chapter, the Meditation Bead, at least in a small way, can help us to fight our loss of focus and spiritual drifting.

Meditations are more than simply thinking about different aspects of each mystery. According to the *Catechism of the Catholic Church* (§2708), *"Meditation engages thought, imagination, emotion, and desire."*

Contemplating the mysteries allows us to consider what we might do for the spiritual health and growth in our lives as we recall what Jesus and Mary did in theirs. The meditations open up the world of Jesus and Mary to us. They let us consider many aspects of Jesus's life. They also look at Mary's life and, by extension, at St. Joseph and others.

By contrast, instead of looking outward at the events in Jesus's life, the Loveful Mysteries force us to look inside ourselves, specifically at the state of Love within us, primarily through contemplation on Jesus's own words, example, and guidance.

Speaking more generally, the Rosary is only one form of prayer. Sitting in front of the Blessed Sacrament — or even quietly at home — we can talk to God in our own words, or sit quietly to allow God an openness to us. Prayer encompasses much. It is not restricted to the Rosary or to formulaic prayers, although they are all important and powerful. There are many opportunities for communication with God.

In part, Our Lady's Medjugorje message of April 25, 2022 repeated a frequent call from Our Lady: *"Dear children! I am looking at you and I see that you are lost. That is why I am calling all of you: return to God, return to prayer..."*

## THE LOVEFUL MYSTERIES
==========================
### Part Two
==========================

For a very long time, Our Lady has been trying to help us in her numerous apparitions, especially over the past 200 years. She has changed the path of many of us, bringing us back to God.

But far too many have either not heard her words, or have heard them, but then blindly turned back to the distractions of the world.

To make matters worse, others, especially a number of non-Catholic Christian sects, are intent on keeping people from listening to Our Lady at all — no matter how solid is the evidence that she has been, and still is, with us. They wrongly tell people that they should restrict themselves to reading Scripture and only pray to Jesus — but certainly not talk to or listen to Our Lady and the saints. Even prayers to God the Father Himself can be given short shrift by some other churches.

They often do this by twisting the words or context of Scripture, of history, and of Catholic teachings themselves. Therefore, the urgent warnings and help that Our Lady has been giving to us for centuries — especially in recent times — never reach many people.

••••••

We know that love is important, but why is it so important as to warrant its own mysteries of the Rosary?

In part, paragraph 1829 of the Catechism of the Catholic Church says, *"The* fruits *of charity are joy, peace, and mercy."*

Referring to St. Augustine, that same paragraph adds that love as the fulfillment of our works is the goal. We read, *"There is the goal; that is why we run: we run toward it, and once we reach it, in it we shall find rest."*

For simplicity, we'll look at three messages given by Our Lady in her apparitions at Medjugorje over one six-week period.

I won't be spending time on the background and massive good that has come out of Our Lady's apparitions at Medjugorje.[25] There are many sources available elsewhere for that. Instead, I will look here at the specific messages of Our Lady from February through March 2020.

For decades, Our Lady has been giving messages to the world from Medjugorje on the 25th of each month. For many years before March 2020, she also gave messages to the visionary Mirjana on the 2nd of each month.[26] At the time of this writing, Mirjana still receives a message from Our Lady annually on the 18th of March.

On March 18, 2020, Our Lady told Mirjana that she would no longer be giving messages on the 2nd of each month.

Then, at the end of that March 18th message, Our Lady added this: *"Without love, there is no salvation."*

In some earlier messages over the years, Our Lady had effectively said the same thing. However, there was no previous statement regarding love being critical for salvation as concise and direct as that one:

"*Without love, there is no salvation.*"

Although more direct, this is consistent with the Catechism of the Catholic Church (§1813) when it refers to the three theological virtues — including charity [love].

The Catechism says this:

[The theological virtues — faith, hope, and charity] *"...are infused by God into the souls of the faithful to make them capable of acting as his children* and of meriting eternal life." *(Emphasis added.)*

To many people, charity has a sense of love in action. Love itself, of which there are several kinds, often carries a sense of

---

[25] *See the Preface regarding the events in Medjugorje.*

[26] *Originally meant primarily for unbelievers, defined as those who have not yet experienced God's love, in 2004, Our Lady then said that the messages on the 2nd of the month were for everyone. These messages had, in large part, a special connection to the importance of love from God and within ourselves.*

feeling or emotion. In reality, when done from the heart, charity and love are one.

Compare the importance of love here with numerous Scripture passages including 1 John 4:7: *"Beloved, let us love one another, because love is from God. Everyone who loves is born of God and knows God."*

We also see this in 1 John 4:16: *"...God is love, and whoever abides in love abides in God, and God in him."*

And this passage in 1 Corinthians 13:13: *"Thus there are three things that endure: faith, hope, and love, and the greatest of these is love."*

There are many other passages concerning the importance of love in Scripture. (For example, see the famous passage at 1 Corinthians 13:4-7.)

Since the 1980s, I have been closely involved with Mary's messages from Medjugorje. Without suggesting that other things aren't important, I believe that some people can get so distracted by the details, the many trees, that they sometimes lose the simple, but urgent awareness of the larger forest — which is made up of the messages given to the world.

Because of my close and exclusive interest in the messages, something new, even an apparent change in tone, has often been especially noticeable to me. After that March 18, 2020 message combined with a couple of previous messages, I remembered feeling a bit shaken.

Love was always important to Mary and has often been mentioned in her messages. The word love might appear several times in a message[27]. Other times, the word love does not appear at all. But, in this case, something felt distinctly different.

I hadn't studied the messages in context at the time. Still, I couldn't forget the uneasy feeling that something was different. Nonetheless, I did nothing further about it until I was asked to speak for the 40th Anniversary of Our Lady's apparitions in June 2021. I would be speaking about the

---

[27] *In at least 26 messages, some form of the word love appeared from ten to fourteen times. Yet, in the context of the many hundreds of messages in well over 40 years, that is a very small percentage of messages with higher number counts.*

Loveful Mysteries.

As a reminder, the Loveful Mysteries did not originate in Medjugorje.

> *A comment on origins: Those who pray the Rosary do not do so because of its history, but because of the strength of its prayers, its spiritual connection to God and Our Lady, its mantle of protection, and the power the Rosary can have in our lives.*
>
> *The story of the origins of the Loveful Mysteries does not affect their use anymore than does the background of other mysteries. Although some will ask, their story is not discussed in this edition of the book.*

As part of the preparation for my talk about the Loveful Mysteries, I went back to look at the message of March 18, 2020. Messages from Our Lady are generally not long. Although some may be longer or shorter, many are just the length of one or two short paragraphs.[28]

I was surprised when I found that the word love appeared in that March 18 message not once, not five times, but *nine times* in the message that ended by unambiguously stating, *"Without love, there is no salvation."*[29]

Sixteen days earlier, on March 2, was the last message Our Lady gave on the second of the month. I went back to look at that message. Did that message also mention love? It did. How many times did the word love appear in the message of March 2, 2020?

Nine times.

That was remarkable to me. In just over two weeks, two messages in a row contained the word exactly nine times. It seemed to be no coincidence.

As Our Lady announced that she would be ending her

---

[28] *The March 18 message contains about 12 sentences without the regular closing farewell. Count depends on translation and grammatical formatting.*

[29] *For context, the final sentence says, "Like my Son, I am also saying to you: love each other because without love there is no salvation."*

messages on the second of each month, she apparently felt that it was critical not only to tell us how important love is, but also to give what seemed to me to be a warning. Her warning seemed to be that we are not loving enough — and that our shortcoming is serious.

*An Aside: God is Love, and we can't be with God without real love, love from the heart. So exactly how literally should we consider the fact that God actually is love?*

*In 1 John 4:8, the Apostle John tells us,* "Whoever does not know love does not know God, because God is love." *Section 221 of the Catechism of the Catholic Church says, in part,* "God's very being is love." *Repeating John, section 214 of the Catechism says,* "God is Love." *[Emphases added.]*

*Few fully consider what this actually means when they think about God.*

I went back one more month. Would the message of February 2, 2020, also mention love? It did.

*Nine times — again.*

In three messages, in just over six weeks, the word love appeared 27 times. Even without having made a close examination of the messages at that time, no wonder I had been uneasy. For Our Lady, love had become dominant above almost all else — other than prayer itself. Nonetheless, this is not meant to diminish the numerous other significant teachings from Our Lady during her many years of apparitions.

What about the messages to the world on the 25$^{th}$ of February and 25$^{th}$ of March 2020?

Zero.

The word love did not appear even once.

Merely counting the number of times the word "love" appears in messages may seem to be a simplistic way to make such judgments. Nonetheless, it does give us at least a general suggestion of its importance.

The author could not find any six-week period nearly as high as the 27 times love appeared in the messages from

February 2, 2020, through March 18, 2020.

Even though the Loveful Mysteries do not directly connect to Medjugorje, the author believes that their importance is strongly supported both in light of the messages from Our Lady and in Scripture itself.

••••••

So how are we to look at ourselves, our strength of love, our unselfish love that is (or should be) truly from the heart — a total love of God and of our neighbor as ourselves?

Mostly, the vast majority of us find it difficult to examine our personal ability to love adequately. It's not likely that most of us truly love enough — especially with an honest and genuine love from the heart.

Sure, we know that love is important. We hear it all the time. We know that we *should* love. Of course, we *do* love as we are able. But Our Lady appears to say that it may be too little. In reality, a true love of God and our neighbor may not be deep within most of us at all.

Should we blame ourselves for that? The virtues and gifts of real love aren't always easy to nurture. Nonetheless, we should be aware of our need for it in God. We should consistently work to understand it and to grow the love which Jesus demands of us. We must ask God for more love within us and work to put it into practice in our daily lives.

Attention to little things can eventually lead to the love we are tasked to have for both God and for each other. We must learn to be careful and loveful in our actions and words.

Words are a critical part of love. So are our actions. Love is not always easy.

••••••

Although the other mysteries of the Rosary do let us look at ourselves, the Loveful Mysteries have a primary purpose to look at the love of Jesus, to look at what Jesus tells us in Scripture, and to let us meditate on how much we may be falling short. Only by having this awareness closely in front of us do we have any chance of strengthening the love within us, of becoming closer to God — to God, who *is* Love.

Meditating on the Loveful Mysteries is one way to help us do that.

••••

*An Important Aside:* In *Understanding Divine Mercy* (Marian Press; 2021), Father Chris Alar, MIC, a Marian Father of the Immaculate Conception, writes: *"We associate God with love because it is the most supreme of all virtues."*

Father Alar also tells us this:

> *"We have different modes of love, but the greatest mode of love is mercy. Mercy is the highest form of the highest virtue — you can't do better. If you want to get to heaven, the surest and best way is to be merciful as the Heavenly Father is merciful (see Lk 6:36). Accept God's mercy and return it to your neighbor."*

Later, Father Alar quotes Father Seraphim Michalenko (1930-2021) who defined mercy as: *"Loving the unlovable and forgiving the unforgivable."*[30]

We must trust in God's mercy. Divine Mercy is more critical than most are aware.

It is important that we understand mercy and the message of the Divine Mercy. St. John Paul II felt strongly about it. On August 17, 2002, he "entrusted the world to Divine Mercy." It was just two months later, on October 16, 2002, that St. John Paul II presented the Luminous Mysteries of the Rosary.

Pope Benedict XVI called Divine Mercy "the nucleus of the Gospel."

Father Alar ties it in further when he writes, *"...the message of Divine Mercy is not optional, because it is the 'nucleus' of the Gospel, and living the message is necessary*

---

[30] *The beloved Father Seraphim Michalenko (1930-2021), MIC, served as vice-postulator in St. Faustina's cause for canonization in North America.*

*to get to heaven."*

Too many dismiss important tools for spirituality, including the Rosary, as not really required, as optional. That is a mistake. Father Alar cautions us: *"The devotion to Divine Mercy is a devotion to God, and devotion to God is not optional."*

Do you know enough about the Divine Mercy and the importance of Divine Mercy Sunday? If not, determine to learn about it soon.

Along with other books and resources, Father Alar's book is recommended if you wish to learn more about Divine Mercy.

Note that the author of the book in your hands believes that the Divine Mercy may be an answer to our entreaty in the Fatima Prayer.

Surmising only, to the author, it seems that Jesus might be answering us saying: *Yes, I will have mercy. All you need to do is trust in Me and I will do it. Even so, through the Chaplet of the Divine Mercy, also ask my Father.*

Of course, trusting in Jesus means more than just saying the words. It means that we must *actually* have trust in Jesus.

Pray.

••••

Returning to meditations on what Jesus has told us in Scripture, we remember that we should also work to uncover the childlike love of Jesus and His Father that children have, that many of us had when we were children.

Unless we change to become like little children, we will not enter the kingdom of heaven (see Matthew 18:3; Mark 10:14; Luke 18:16). Jesus knows that most of us do not have the simplicity of being childlike in both faith and love — but we need to find it.

In truth, the thinking and feelings of children are often not as simple or immature as many people think.

Little children love on a simpler and different level than do most adults. It is generally love without question or analysis. Analysis is often the antithesis of simplicity. Children brought up knowing Jesus, don't analyze. They just believe. They just love.

> *"Amen, I say to you, whoever does not receive the kingdom of God like a little child will never enter it."* [Luke 18:17.]

We should notice the total dependence of children. As little children believe and depend on their parents, so should we believe in and depend upon God.

These mysteries are a tool to look into ourselves. Like most other mysteries, the Loveful Mysteries are scriptural. We are able to spend time meditating on the words and actions of Jesus and His admonitions to us.

For many, the meditations can be especially instructive and introspective. We can work to repair or strengthen the love we should have within us, love for God and also for our neighbor.

Of course, these mysteries are not required for that. Prayer, reading Scripture, regular examinations of conscience while reflecting on our shortcomings and our need to become better — these are all ways we can strengthen our interior selves, including our faith and love.

But, for many, praying the Loveful Mysteries may be of particular help.

For those who can, I also recommend, or at least suggest, spending some time each day reading lives of the saints. The lives of many saints, both declared and undeclared, are compelling stories. They inspire us and provide examples for our own lives.

If you find that you are not advancing in Christian love enough as you pray these mysteries, then find something else to do in order to take action on Our Lady's quiet but direct warning: *"Without Love, there is no Salvation."*

We'll digress a moment for two asides.

*Love Isn't Easy. Too often, do some people get angry with others. Their concerns are often over things that aren't worth getting upset about — and that can't be changed anyway.*

*If you're angry, you can't be at peace. Being at peace is more important than being right. We would all be surprised to understand how many times we're not actually right anyway. Regardless, do your best to be humble. Be forgiving. Learn to nurture things that really matter.*

*Pray. Ask God to be with you. Seek forgiveness for yourself from others when you have been angry with them. For most people, none of this is easy. Nonetheless, do your best to find inner and family peace through faith and prayer and forgiveness. When you find that peace, nurture it with care. It's an important part of loving both God and neighbor.*

••••••

<u>*Understanding Love From The Heart*</u>. *In trying to understand love from the heart, consider the dog.*

*God imbued the dog with unconditional love for us. Largely because of that, and especially in the Western world, many consider the dog to be one of God's great gifts to us.*

*As we love God and our neighbor, can we be a reflection of the love we see and feel, or that, even without having a dog, we know that the dog shows to us unconditionally? Did God give us the dog to offer His own lessons in love from the heart to us each day? Do we pay attention?*

*It's not simply receiving love from a dog with no obligation from us. It's giving back, as we care for and love them. Can we then turn that love firmly to God and to each other? Or do we ignore this example assuming that it's "just a dog." How can a dog seriously teach us anything that we can't know by other means?*

*In the few dogs that do not love, we often find the cause is in us. It's people's errors, sometimes intentional, in breeding, raising, or caring for them. In a similar way, our own love for God and others can be damaged. God doesn't do that. We, the world, and others around us do.*

*We don't need dogs to teach any of this to us, do we? Well, perhaps it's just an easy-to-find example of what we should be doing. Is God able to look at us as having the same unconditional love for Him as the dog has for us?*

*God can whisper to us through His creations.*

*Perhaps we do need the example the dog sets for us after all.*

*As babies, we're all born with love. It's as much a part of us as are our hands and feet and heart. But, along the way, life sometimes damages and buries that love so deeply in a small number of us as to seem to be gone — even though it's still there. But, if it becomes buried deeply enough, we can do much damage to others and to ourselves.*

*Love from the heart is precious. We should continually protect, repair, and grow our love — and support others in doing the same thing when and as we can. Really, we can't always do that, but prayer is always possible.*

*Let's return to the Loveful Mysteries.*

••••••

Another thing in the Loveful Mysteries is different from other mysteries. The 5th Loveful mystery does not reflect an event or even a direct teaching of Jesus. Almost all other Rosary mysteries do.

However, neither do the 4th and 5th Glorious Mysteries. Those reflect two events not specifically found in Scripture: The Assumption and the Crowning of Our Lady as Queen of Heaven and Earth.

The 5th Loveful mystery is also different in that it comes from something that Paul tells us. But Paul is not alone in what he writes in Scripture. The three words of the 5th mystery, *Pray Without Ceasing*, are seen in different forms and contexts elsewhere. But it is those three words that are often best remembered and are frequently quoted.

We find this call to frequent prayer in Mary's near-constant encouragement to pray. A call to frequent prayer is certainly not unique with Paul.

Mary has asked that we pray for her intentions: *"Little Children, I am in need of your prayers. Pray, pray, pray"* [Message to Ivanka on June 25, 2021]. Over many centuries, Mary has told us to pray.

Mary has told us that, with prayer and fasting, even wars can be stopped.[31]

---

[31] *As an example, see the Medjugorje message of January 25, 2001.*

## LOOKING AT EACH LOVEFUL MYSTERY

=========================
Part One
=========================

**The First Loveful Mystery:**

### No Greater Love

*"As the Father has loved me, so have I loved you. Remain in my love. If you keep my commandments, you will remain in my love, just as I have kept my Father's commandments and remain in his love.*

*"I have told you these things so that my joy may be in you and your joy may be complete. This is my commandment: love one another as I have loved you. **No one can have greater love than to lay down his life for his friends.** You are my friends if you do what I command you."* (John 15:9-14. Emphasis added here and in the verses below.)

•••••••••

Jesus laid down His life for us. But what are we willing to do? Are there people or values we know of, right now, for whom or for which we would willingly lay down our own lives? Jesus is clear that there is no greater love than this.

Might we be willing to sacrifice ourselves even for strangers? Many have. Where are our limits? We are called to love even our enemies. (See Matthew 5:43-48.)

Laying down one's life is not done simply to "prove" something. That is not what Jesus did. Our bodies are temples of the Holy Spirit. Therefore, we have an obligation to protect and care for our bodies. Our bodies are not ours alone:

*"We are stewards, not owners, of the life God has entrusted to us. It is not ours to dispose of."* [Catechism of the Catholic Church §2280.]

Laying down one's life is done for a specific and consequential reason, often to save the life of another. People may willingly lay down their lives as they stand up for their faith in God, for Jesus, for their Church. Lives are given in defense of country or for ideals such as liberty, freedom, and human rights.

Such sacrifices happen even today. People throughout the world have to make difficult choices as they and their families are faced with threats and intimidation by the likes of terrorists, violent criminals, and totalitarian regimes.

Evil people and oppressive governments do all they can to force people to renounce their faith and their beliefs.

This can happen even outside of totalitarian regimes. In recent times, rights and freedoms have been taken away in what were formerly considered to be free countries. This has happened in countries in Europe. This has also been happening in America. The world is not safe.

This calling to love and sacrifice does not always entail actually laying down one's life. For most of us, that choice never arises. Rather, it is the unselfish *willingness,* as well as the actuality, of giving our life for another person that is important, regardless of actually having to do it. There is *no greater love* than this.

We also remember that *"...whoever wishes to save his life will lose it, but whoever loses his life for my sake will save it."* [Luke 9:24.]

Such willing sacrifice can be given out of love for a fellow human being, even if a total stranger — or out of love for God Himself.

As doctors' descriptions of the passion and death of Jesus show, Jesus suffered horrendously as He lay down His life for our sins. No one else could have done that for us. Jesus did not need to "prove" anything.

In the vast majority of cases, United States Congressional Medal of Honor winners laid down their lives, or undertook actions that could have led to the loss of their lives for their friends, for their comrades-in-arms.

Many saints and martyrs also laid down their lives for others — or for their love of God. Parents have laid their lives down for their children. Mothers have sacrificed their lives even for their unborn children.

How far is each of us willing to go?

In many cases, people may have just minutes, per- haps

mere seconds, to decide whether they are willing to step in and lay down their life for another.

In the case of Jesus, He knew well in advance what He would be doing. During the Agony in the Garden — the First Sorrowful Mystery — Jesus asked His Father to let pass what He knew was coming.

*"In his anguish, he prayed so fervently that his sweat became like great drops of blood falling on the ground."* [Luke 22:44.]

But Jesus submitted to what was to come. Jesus laid His life down voluntarily. Wholly innocent, he endured terrible sufferings for us.

There are certainly cases when people have known in advance that they would be sacrificing their lives for another. Knowing what is coming far in advance can be especially difficult.

The sufferings of Jesus were more intense than what most people understand. Jesus knew this even before He was born in Bethlehem. The Sorrowful mysteries and the Loveful mysteries, especially the First Loveful Mystery, are certainly linked together.

To further solidify the importance of this First Mystery, we read in 1 John 3:16 (NCB):

*This is how we know what love is: he laid down his life for us, and we in turn must be prepared to lay down our lives for our brethren.*


## The Second Loveful Mystery:

### Whatever You Do For One (you do for Me)

In Matthew:

*"Then the King will say to those on his right, 'Come, you who are blessed by my Father, inherit the kingdom prepared for you from the foundation of the world. For I was hungry and you gave me something to eat; I was*

*thirsty and you gave me something to drink; I was a stranger and you welcomed me; I was naked and you clothed me; I was ill and you took care of me; I was in prison and you came to visit me.'*

*"Then the righteous will say to him, 'Lord, when did we see you hungry and give you something to eat, or thirsty and give you something to drink? When did we see you a stranger and welcome you, or naked and clothe you? When did we see you ill or in prison and come to visit you?' And the King will answer, 'Amen, I say to you,* **whatever you did for one** *of the least of these brethren of mine,* **you did for me.** *"'* (Matthew 25:34-40.)

In John:

*"I give you a new commandment: love one another. Just as I have loved you, so you should also love one another. This is how everyone will know that you are my disciples: if you love one another."* (John 13:34-35.)

•••••••••

Do we do enough for others whom we see each day? Do we do enough for others whom we don't see but who we nonetheless know need help? It isn't necessary to help the whole world, just those whom we can. These may personally cross into our lives, or we may become aware of someone not near to us, but in real need nonetheless.

Are we really able to decide that someone will not get our help? None are unlimited in resources, and we all know that some in the world will abuse our charity. However, many do need our help. Are we really able to choose wisely? Do we even have a choice? Or do we simply help all who we can and leave what happens afterward up to God? We cannot — nor are we called — to help everyone.

It's not always easy. There is danger in the world of which we should be aware.

We try to make good decisions, but God chooses. Are we listening?

If we're not open to helping those who come in front of us, we will surely miss times when what we failed to do for others was, in reality, a failure to do it for Jesus Himself. Although we should be reasonable and thoughtful in our actions, we must always be aware that whatever we do for one of the least of His brethren, we do for Him.

In this mystery, we are told to be *doers* of the Word, not just believers, not just talkers, not just listeners. This mystery can strengthen love in our daily lives more than any other.

However, to have the spirituality that we want to achieve, love must come from the heart. Such gifts of the heart are best given with even the briefest prayer inside of us. In this Second Mystery, meditation and contemplation on the mystery are of particular value in increasing the awareness and strength of love within us.

We end consideration of this mystery with 1 John 3:18:

*Dear children, let us love not in word or speech but in deed and truth.*

What else can we do for Jesus? He tells us to keep His commandments.

## The Third Loveful Mystery:

### The Greatest Commandment

*"Teacher, which is the greatest commandment in the Law?" Jesus said to him, " 'You shall love the Lord your God with all your heart, and with all your soul, and with all your mind.'* **This is the greatest and the first commandment.** *The second is like it: 'You shall love your neighbor as yourself.' Everything in the Law and the Prophets depends on these two commandments."* (Matthew 22:36-40.)

•••••••••

Jesus makes it clear that it is not the Ten Commandments, but the Love of God that is the first and greatest commandment. The second is to love our neighbors as ourselves. Note that *the whole law* depends on these two commandments.

The Old Testament counterpart to this is in Deuteronomy:

*"You shall love the Lord, your God, with all your heart, and with all your soul, and with all your might."* [Deuteronomy 6:5.]

Deuteronomy continues:

*"You shall keep these things that I command you today in your heart. Teach them to your children. You shall talk of them when you are sitting in your home, and when you are walking along the way, and when you lie down and when you rise up."* [Deuteronomy 6:6-7.] [32]

All these things in Deuteronomy are given as commands, not suggestions. They are not merely good things to do. As we specifically read in verse 6 above, we are told that they are commands. So is what we are told in Matthew above.[33]

How strong is our love for God? If we can't love our neighbor who is in front of us and whom we can see, is it not more difficult to love God whom we cannot see?

Aren't these two things — love of God and love of neighbor — linked, as we read in Matthew?

For more again, we turn to 1 John 5:2-3:

*This is how we know that we love the children of God: by loving God and obeying his commandments. For the love of God is this: that we keep his commandments.*

Further, we are told that God is love itself.

This third mystery also links to the Sorrowful Mysteries in

---

[32] *Judaism looks at this section in a more expansive context. Nonetheless, this directive in Deuteronomy reminds us of our responsibilities to pass the commandments of God to our children. It also reminds us of the things commanded in Scripture.*

[33] *I add that some debate the understanding of a command in Scripture as somewhat nuanced. Nonetheless, here we should be working to fulfill this important and repeated Scriptural command to love God.*

that Jesus did His Father's will regardless of what Jesus wanted. He did it out of unconditional love for His Father — and as love for us.

What do we need to do to change ourselves so that God permeates our whole being and our whole life every day? Might that also let us take better care of each other?

A contemplation on the full gamut of love within us is found in these first three Loveful Mysteries.

## The Fourth Loveful Mystery:

### The Beatitudes
[Any one or more, or all of them.]

The fourth and fifth Loveful Mysteries change to other elements of spirituality, while including continuing aspects of love. In the Beatitudes, we find multiple opportunities to contemplate love.

### The Beatitudes
[Matthew 5:1-12.]

The Sermon on the Mount. *When Jesus saw the crowds, he went up on the mountain. After he was seated, his disciples gathered around him. Then he began to teach them as follows:*

[From here on is Matthew 5:3-12, also from The New Catholic Bible. When possible, it's good to read these verses after announcing the mystery.]

### The Beatitudes.
*"Blessed are the poor in spirit, for theirs is the kingdom of heaven.*
*Blessed are those who mourn, for they will be comforted.*
*Blessed are the meek, for they will inherit the earth.*
*Blessed are those who hunger and thirst for justice, for they will have their fill.*
*Blessed are the merciful, for they will obtain mercy.*
*Blessed are the pure of heart, for they will see God.*

*Blessed are the peacemakers, for they will be called children of God.*

*Blessed are those who are persecuted in the cause of justice, for theirs is the kingdom of heaven.*

*Blessed are you when people insult you and persecute you and utter all kinds of calumnies* [verbal falsehoods or verbal abuse] *against you for my sake. Rejoice and be glad, for your reward will be great in heaven. In the same manner, they persecuted the prophets who preceded you."*

•••••••••

Meditations on the fourth mystery can focus on a single Beatitude, on more than one, or on all of them. However, to maintain quality prayer, it is often best to limit meditations to no more than one or two Beatitudes. As serve the needs of those praying, they can be the same or a different beatitude (or beatitudes) each time the decade is prayed.

Note that *Blessed Are The Merciful* (Matthew 5:7) fits especially well with the Loveful Mysteries. Mercy is a particularly valued form of love. Twice in Scripture, Jesus tells us to consider these words: *"I desire mercy and not sacrifice."*[34]

However, all Beatitudes have great value.

This mystery appears to depart from others. Other mysteries of the Rosary are simple, single events in Scripture or, in the Loveful Mysteries, a scriptural teaching. This Fourth Loveful Mystery is indeed a single event — the Sermon on the Mount. However, there is more than one teaching in the Beatitudes themselves.

Most people have at least a loose familiarity with the often-quoted Beatitudes. Although they may have been forgotten through lack of use, some people even memorized them when they were younger. Sadly, others seem to have never heard them at all.

Of course, it is still praiseworthy to memorize the Beatitudes along with other important or favorite verses from

---

[34] *See Matthew 9:13 and Matthew 12:7 .*

Scripture.

As we heard earlier, St. John Paul II recommended reading related passages of Scripture when mysteries of the Rosary are announced. Here, it is especially helpful to do so. This is especially important when the Loveful Mysteries are prayed in a public setting.

As already mentioned, rather than meditating on all or other Beatitudes, one might choose: *Blessed are the merciful, for they will obtain mercy.* For many people, it is the most commonly known.

Recall what we heard about mercy in an earlier section. Father Seraphim Michalenko defined mercy as: *"Loving the unlovable and forgiving the unforgivable."*

Is that not real love? This one beatitude alone makes the Beatitudes worthy of their own mystery. But the Beatitudes can do even more for us. Understanding them can aid in spiritual maturity. Nonetheless, the qualities of mercy in the Beatitudes are directly linked to love.

*"The quality of mercy ... is twice blest. It blesseth him that gives and him that takes:'Tis mightiest in the mightiest; it becomes the throned monarch better than his crown..."* (Shakespeare's *Merchant of Venice*, 1597, Act IV, Scene 1.)

Other virtues in the Beatitudes can also put us in a frame of mind — a frame of spirit — to love. Perhaps that is another reason we find them in these mysteries.

*AN ASIDE ABOUT VIRTUE:* The *Catechism of the Catholic Church* (§1803) defines a virtue as *"an habitual and firm disposition to do the good. It allows the person not only to perform good acts, but to give the best of himself."*

More formally, the three theological virtues are those of Faith, Hope, and Charity [Love]. These are gifts from God. They are what we pray for — and are good to announce — before each of the three associated Hail Marys as the Rosary begins ["for faith," "for hope," "for charity" (which is love)].

The *Catechism of the Catholic Church* says that the three theological virtues *"inform all the moral virtues and give life to them."*

For a discussion of these three virtues that open the Rosary, see the *Catechism of the Catholic Church,* paragraphs 1812 through 1829. You'll find a list of other virtues there, too.

Spirituality is strengthened by developing virtues and putting them into practice.

••••••

The teachings of Jesus continue beyond the Beatitudes in Chapter Five of Matthew. Wisdom urges a full reading, with meditation, on the rest of Chapter Five — as well as on the teachings of Jesus throughout all four Gospels of Scripture.

As we meditate on what we read in Scripture, we see the importance of love throughout His teachings. We can also see the importance of prayer in helping us to understand what Jesus tells us — and how to apply those teachings in our daily lives.

As a single example, we might consider whether we practice enough forgiveness and mercy towards others. Perhaps we can better understand how God looks at us, too.

Paragraph 1820 in the *Catechism of the Catholic Church* says this about the Beatitudes:

*Christian hope unfolds from the beginning of Jesus' preaching in the proclamation of the beatitudes. The beatitudes raise our hope toward heaven as the new Promised Land; they trace the path that leads through the trials that await the disciples of Jesus.*

Through the Beatitudes, we continue to meditate on our personal virtues — or lack of them — and what we might do to grow spiritually. Within each of them is help to grow the love and spiritual strength within us. We might also understand the Beatitudes as a promise of caring from God to us. We can reflect on them as an aid in understanding, appreciating, and caring about others. As we grow spiritually, we grow closer to God. We not only give our love to God, but also to others who enter into our lives.

What are we doing each day to develop or strengthen the spiritual and moral virtues in our lives? This mystery lets us consider that.

## The Fifth Loveful Mystery:

### Pray Without Ceasing

In First Thessalonians, we read:

> *Rejoice always;* **pray continually***; give thanks in all circumstances; for this is the will of God for you in Christ Jesus.* [1 Thessalonians 5:16-18.]

Note that *"pray continually"* is translated elsewhere, and more commonly remembered as: *"pray without ceasing."* For all practical purposes, the meaning is the same.

In Chapter 11 of Mark, we find this:

> *Jesus said to them, "Have faith in God. Amen, I say to you, whoever says to this mountain, 'Be lifted up and thrown into the sea,' and does not doubt in his heart but believes that what he says will happen, it will be accomplished for him. So I tell you, whatever you ask for in prayer, believe that you have received it, and it will be yours.*
> *"And whenever you stand in prayer, forgive whatever grievance you have against anybody, so that your Father in heaven may forgive your wrongs too."* [Mark 11:22-25.]

·········

Prayer is mentioned many times in Scripture. Recall the parable in Luke 18:1 where Luke advises that we *"pray always without becoming weary."*

Many, many times, Our Lady at Medjugorje has said to *"pray, pray, pray."* As part of her message of December 4, 1986, Our Lady talked about recognizing evil and allowing the Lord to purify our hearts. She counseled, *"Therefore, dear children,* **pray without ceasing** *and prepare your hearts in penance and fasting."*

In her January 1, 1987 message, we find the same call to

prayer: *"Therefore, dear children, **pray without ceasing**...."*

On May 25, 1988, we read, *"**Never cease praying** so that Satan cannot take advantage of you."*

On August 25, 1989, there is this: *"Therefore, little children, **pray, pray, pray!** Let prayers begin to rule in the whole world."*

On September 25, 1990, this: *"Dear children! I invite you to **pray with the heart** in order that your prayer may be a conversation with God."* [Emphasis added in each of the above.]

Over and over and over, throughout the decades of her apparitions, Our Lady has told us to pray, to pray from the heart, and to pray without ceasing. Such has it been even at her other apparitions over the centuries.

Those who want to better love God the Father, His Son, Jesus, and the Holy Spirit — one God, the Holy Trinity — can become closer to each of them, separately and together, through prayer.

Some may not consider this, but real prayer to God from the heart is with love. Love and prayer can become as one. One might not even be aware of it but, with ongoing prayer, love grows.

•••••••••

What does it mean to "pray continually" or to "pray without ceasing?" Does it mean to pray constantly every moment of the day, waking up frequently at night to pray even more? It does not mean that. Even Our Lady does not mean it that literally.

Were I to tell you that I *always* eat broccoli (I don't), would you think that I eat broccoli without ceasing, carrying around pieces in my pocket to nibble on throughout the entire day? Would you picture me putting bits in my mouth between breaths as I sleep at night? If I told you that you should *never stop* drinking water, would you assume that I mean to drink water every moment of every day?

You would not. You would know what I meant.

In the same way, praying continuously means that we

should be praying from the heart as often as is practical throughout the day, but not literally without a moment of ceasing. That would not be possible.

Our Lady did ask us to pray three hours a day — not continuously every minute of every day. Substantive daily prayer is the goal that Our Lady has set for us.

Okay. Don't panic. You certainly don't have to pray three hours a day as you get started. You might have trouble praying even for 30 minutes. Just do the best you can. Some prayer — hopefully from the heart — is better than no prayer. Then grow from there. Just pray.

Yes, I know you're busy and that you have a life. Our Lady knows that, too. But don't let the less necessary things of the world keep you so busy that you don't pray at all.

Remember God. Set your priorities accordingly.

Set appropriate alarms or electronic reminders during the day if it helps you not to forget prayer.

Many saints offer examples of the importance of praying "without ceasing" and what it can mean.

Sometime before the year 1234, Blessed Jordan of Saxony wrote that St. Dominic was *"ceaselessly devoted to prayer."*[35] We know from Scripture that Jesus Himself spent much time praying and fasting.

Importantly, prayer and fasting often go together.

At Medjugorje, Our Lady has suggested fasting (with prayer) on bread and water on Wednesdays and Fridays.

When people refer to saying a Rosary, they generally mean five decades of the Rosary. But that is not actually a (full) Rosary. Until revised, saying the original fifteen decades — Joyful, Sorrowful, Glorious — is generally still considered a full Rosary. Saying all 20 or 25 decades (if you choose to add the Luminous and also the Loveful Mysteries) might become defined as a full Rosary in the future, but it isn't now —

---

[35] *From* The Life of Saint Dominic *by Bede Jarrett, O.P., Cluny Media 2018 edition of the original text.*

although perhaps it should be.[36]

A (full) daily Rosary is recommended by the Church, by saints, and by Our Lady. Those who complain that some set of mysteries is just said one day a week will be gratified to understand that *all* mysteries can be prayed every day of the week. [When saying Rosary mysteries beyond five, it is not necessary to repeat the opening prayers of the Rosary as you begin the next sets of mysteries.]

Note that the Fatima seer, Sister Lucia, gave a formula for a pledge for peace.[37] The second part of the pledge does not say that a full daily Rosary is always necessary. The pledge says, *"To say part of the Rosary (five decades) daily while meditating on the mysteries."* Nonetheless, we should pray beyond five decades daily when we can. But just do whatever you are able to do.

St. John Paul II noted that praying a *full* Rosary, including the newer mysteries, isn't always easy and that we should just do what we can.

As we will see in a moment, we can make much of our daily life a prayer, even apart from our formal prayers.

Luke cautioned that we should be on our guard that our hearts do not become weighed down with the anxieties of daily life. He added that we must *"Be vigilant at all times, praying for the strength to survive all those things that will take place and to stand in the presence of the Son of Man."* [Luke 21:34-36.]

Can we stay vigilant through prayer? Is our daily connection to God strong enough? In addition to our personal prayers, we must listen for the Voice of God. God's voice can come to us at any time in our lives.

But listen carefully. God might be whispering.

---

[36] *Regarding the definition of a full Rosary, most Church references to fifteen decades as a full Rosary were already in place even before St. John Paul II presented the Luminous Mysteries. One example of such a Church reference is the* Manual of Indulgences *which still identifies fifteen decades as a full Rosary (see Grant #17).*

[37] *From* The True Story of Fatima *(~1947) by John de Marchi, I.M.C.*

## LOOKING AT EACH LOVEFUL MYSTERY
========================
Part Two
========================

How far can we go toward making our life a prayer? The Church has given us help for this in a remarkable doctrine. It comes by way of an often maligned — even by the clergy — and little understood teaching: the Doctrine of Indulgences.

Some might think that this is an unusual moment to link them to our concern for prayer. It is actually quite appropriate. That's because the underlying sense of indulgences — raising our minds and hearts to God — is that of prayer, often through indulgenced activities in reparation for remaining punishment due for our sins.

The current *Manual of Indulgences* is recommended to readers. There are many opportunities for spiritual development within its pages. Converts to Catholicism might be surprised to hear that indulgences even exist today, but they have been around for many centuries. Despite a time of past misunderstandings and abuses by some (later corrected), this remains a powerful doctrine. When used in accordance with the Manual, they can greatly aid us in obtaining holiness, grace, and more.

Indulgences help us to make up for punishment due for *forgiven* sins. A partial indulgence adds an equal amount of grace to the grace we might receive when performing an indulgenced action listed in the *Manual of Indulgences*. A plenary indulgence does even more but is not discussed here.

Many non-Catholics believe that because Christ died for our sins, all sins, together with their related punishments, are forgiven. Martin Luther was upset about the abuse of indulgences by some in the Church during his time, but even he didn't believe that.

You can only receive the grace of an indulgence for yourself or for souls in purgatory, not for another living person. You can pray for other living people. You can ask that God's grace be given to others. You just can't get an indulgence for someone else.

What kind of things can we do? There are many things

listed in the *Manual of Indulgences*. The first general grant of indulgences broadly says that we can merit a partial indulgence by:

*"...carrying out [our] duties and enduring the hardships of life, [raising our] minds in humble trust to God and [making], at least mentally, some pious invocation."*

Even though that is more difficult than it might sound, that covers a lot of life for us, indeed most of what we do in our daily lives.

Our duties include not just our required duties at work or on a job, but may also include duties at home, even in our family relationships.

The *Manual of Indulgences* also tells us:

*"Should someone be devout and zealous enough to fill the day with such acts, he would justly merit, over and above the increase of grace, a fuller remission of punishment, and he can bring in his charity more abundant aid to the souls in purgatory."* [From the Introduction to The Four General Concessions, *Manual of Indulgences,* 1999.]

That one sentence puts into perspective the power of indulgenced grants. It is not merely an indulgence that is the final goal. The increase in devoutness and zealous spirituality through a properly undertaken activity rises above the activity itself. It creates an ongoing awareness of God, an atmosphere of total prayer in one's life, and an openness to God's grace. An indulgence is one means, one tool, on the road to a life of prayer, although it is beneficial even unto itself.

Looking at this single grant of a partial indulgence, we are also told that, in addition to the desire for the indulgence, we should frequently raise our minds "in humble trust" to God.

•••••••••

As assistance in raising our minds to God, we can say, aloud or mentally, a pious invocation in harmony with the performance of an indulgenced action. Among many others, such brief pious invocations might include:

*Praised be Jesus Christ! My God! I hope in you! Your will be done! Heart of Jesus, all for you. Heart of Jesus, in you I trust. Lord, increase our faith. My Lord and my God! (That is as per Thomas's exclamation in John 20:28.) Teach me to do your will, for you are my God. Holy Mary, Mother of God, pray for me. Tender heart of Mary, be my safety!*

Those are just examples. There are indeed countless others found in the *Manual of Indulgences* as well as in many prayer books.

To more fully understand the use of pious invocations, read the opening paragraphs in the appendix on "Pious Invocations" in the *Manual of Indulgences*.

Picture yourself in your daily life, periodically raising your mind to God, perhaps in a simple awareness of His presence, trusting in Him, while acknowledging your spiritual connection by way of some pious invocation. We gradually realize that our lives can indeed become a prayer.

•••••••••

As we already heard, "Praying without ceasing" isn't meant literally. However, you can also see how, with substantive formal daily prayer, perhaps including daily Mass (when available) and the Rosary, combined with even just that one grant of indulgence, your life can move closer to God's encompassing love for us and an increase in our own love for Him.

St. John Paul II noted this connection when he wrote, *"The Rosary, in its own particular way, is part of this varied panorama of 'ceaseless' prayer."*[38]

That ongoing awareness of the presence of God and of God's will, can lead to greater faith, whether for the first time, or by strengthening the faith already within us.

---

[38] *From the* Apostolic Letter, Rosarium Virginis Mariae Of The Supreme Pontiff John Paul II, *Chapter One (13), October 16, 2002.*

Keep in mind that this is just one indulgenced grant from the Manual. There are many others. There is also important spiritual guidance there, even without indulgences, that can lead us to a better understanding of a life of grace and a greater love of God.

I recommend obtaining and reading the *Manual of Indulgences.*

Therefore, in calling us to pray without ceasing, the Fifth Loveful Mystery suggests that we have the opportunity to become continually closer to God by raising our hearts to God frequently throughout the day — to God who *is* Love.

•••••••••

For those saying just five decades of the Rosary a day, the Loveful Mysteries are suggested for Saturdays. The reason is that these mysteries follow the Sorrowful Mysteries (Fridays) to which, as we will see shortly, the Loveful Mysteries connect so well. The Loveful Mysteries end with a strong call to prayer. That leads us directly to the Glorious Mysteries (Sundays).

The Loveful Mysteries begin with *No Greater Love.* That mystery is clearly close to the final mystery of the Passion of Our Lord in the Sorrowful Mysteries. There is certainly no greater love than Jesus had in coming down to us, enduring great suffering, and, finally, giving His life for our sins.

For those who might complain that they want to pray the Joyful Mysteries on Saturdays, there's no problem. The Joyful Mysteries can be prayed every day with the full Rosary or whenever you wish. Remember that a full daily Rosary contains all of the mysteries.

If you prefer, you can pray the Loveful Mysteries on another day of your choosing or add them to mysteries on other days. (You can also choose not to say them at all.) Then you can continue to pray the Joyful Mysteries on both Saturdays and Mondays. It's up to you.

There may also be times when one might choose to say a generic Rosary, with special reflection on each prayer, without the added richness of the mysteries.

*"Sacrifice Your Will." As an aside, meditations are possible on every part of the Our Father as well as on other Rosary prayers. As an example of just one, we consider meditations on "Thy will be done," in the Our Father.*

*In 1916, the Angel of Peace appeared to Lucia, Francisco, and Jacinta, the three children visionaries of Fatima, Portugal. The angel's three apparitions were a prelude to the more famous apparitions of Our Lady of Fatima which came in 1917.*

*Speaking about the angel's second apparition, Father John Horgan says in his book:*[39]

"Then the angel speaks of sacrifices, both those voluntarily undertaken and those the Lord will send to the children... And the angel points out too that the greatest sacrifice of all is the sacrifice of our own will, through acceptance and willing submission to God's plan." [Emphasis added.]

*As another example, during the lesser-known story of reported communications with souls in Purgatory in the 1920s, a seer was told that, to be even better in the eyes of God, she should sacrifice her will.*

*From such repeated counsel, we understand that, if we are to help ourselves (and the souls in Purgatory, as well), we, too, should sacrifice our will. This is found in several places in the diary of Eugenie von der Leyen of Germany.*[40]

*From this, we can consider our own will, our own*

---

[39] *This is from the book,* His Angels at Our Side: Understanding Their Power in Our Souls and the World *by Father John Horgan (2018; EWTN Publishing).*

[40] *The book,* My Discourse With Poor Souls *(1979), by Eugenie von der Leyen, was translated from by Elizabeth Cattana, and published by* The Franciscan Minims of the Perpetual Help of Mary, *Mexico. Examples of such counsel to sacrifice our will are found in diary entries of January 10, 1924, October 2, 1925, and February 6, 1926. Please remember to pray for the souls in Purgatory and to offer Holy Communion for them when you can.*

*choices at each moment of our lives, choices which are sometimes best when we ignore our own will, our own desires, in favor of God's.*

*Therefore, when we pray in the Our Father, "Thy will be done," we should think about, and beyond, those four words, words which are often passed by with little thought and much speed. We have the opportunity to consider God's will versus our own will. There is much more we might consider, even if just tangentially, as we pray those words.*

*This is but one example of how we can slow down and meditate on each prayer of the Rosary.*

•••••

Especially with the addition of mysteries beyond the original 15, St. John Paul II recognized that it will be more difficult for people to say a full Rosary every day. As our lives permit, praying just part of the Rosary daily, perhaps five decades, is often all we can do. As you begin, it can be enough.

As merely a suggestion, one might also consider periodically meditating on both the Sorrowful and Loveful Mysteries together: both first mysteries together, both second mysteries together, etc. Such concurrent mystery meditations can open our hearts to understand even more about both the Passion of Our Lord and ourselves in the light of Love.

Can we learn from each of these corresponding mysteries, one about the other? Can we have an even deeper appreciation for Our Lord's Passion?

In a moment, we will consider this in greater detail.

As already recommended, it is good to consider praying the Chaplet of the Divine Mercy after completing the Rosary, although it can also be prayed separately. The Chaplet of Divine Mercy is just one part of the full Devotion of Divine Mercy.

The Devotion to the Divine Mercy and the messages from Medjugorje are both hope and warnings that time is now limited. It is important that we wait no longer to get our spiritual act together.

So, although the Loveful Mysteries and most else suggested in these pages are optional, getting closer to God is not.

Therefore, many things that might be technically optional aren't really optional anymore than saving our souls is optional. We need to use everything available to us to lead a good life, to love God, and to get to heaven.

Nonetheless, we all have free will. If these things are helpful in your prayer life, use them. If not, pray as you did before they came along.

But pray often and pray from the heart.

•••••••••

Do you have trouble praying? Find a spiritual adviser with whom you are comfortable. Seek advice and counsel in the wisdom of a spiritual priest, deacon, or someone else with strong spirituality.

Remember that Our Lady's answer to prayer being difficult is to pray *more*. Even some of the greatest saints struggled in their faith, but they continued to pray. Having a good spiritual advisor with whom you're comfortable talking is invaluable. Too few people do that today.

•••••••••

On June 19, 2021, Vicka, one of the Medjugorje visionaries, reportedly said:[41]

> *"Our Lady does not ask us to pray the whole day long, but to put prayer at the first place, to put God at the first place, and then perform our works and go ahead in all the aspects of our life, including visiting sick people and other good works.*
>
> *"...When we do a charitable work without prayer, it's not valuable. The same way, when we pray and do not act in a charitable way, it is not valuable either. Those two things, prayer and charity [love], always work together. And then, step-by-step, we go forward."*

---

[41] *As reported at: mysticpost.com/2021/06/message-given-to-ivan-on-19th-june-by-the-queen-of-peace. Accessed 7-25-2021. (See the Preface regarding the events in Medjugorje.)*

# TWO MYSTERIES TOGETHER

When prayed by themselves, the suggested and usual day to pray the Loveful Mysteries is on Saturdays.

However, our meditations can take a different turn by considering two sets of mysteries together. For example, both the Sorrowful and Loveful Mysteries dovetail well together.

One might consider praying these two sets of mysteries, together, on Tuesdays. Or continue as you have always done with each set of mysteries entirely separate — in whichever way your spirituality calls you.

For some, this combined linkage of two sets of mysteries can provide an added level of meditation. When prayed in this way, the pairing of each mystery should be announced together.

Beginning with the First Sorrowful and First Loveful Mysteries, here are brief thoughts on connections between both sets of mysteries when prayed together.

(1st Mysteries) Here is the agony of Jesus's tormenting decision to [Loveful] lay down His life for us as He prays in the Garden [Sorrowful].

(2nd Mysteries) As Jesus endured the scourging for us [Sorrowful], what do we do for Him in our lives today? Cannot we at least do what He asked us to do for others [Loveful] — which we really do for Him?

(3rd Mysteries) With everything else that Jesus suffered, His agony during the horrific crowning with thorns [Sorrowful] showed His total love for His Father as we, too, are asked to do in our hearts, souls, and minds [Loveful].

(4th Mysteries) Fully innocent, Jesus carried the cross on the way to His death, struggling even to walk [Sorrowful]. We are not innocent as we strive to carry and overcome our sinfulness and our failings. We struggle to follow the path of life and virtue that Jesus laid out for us [Loveful] throughout His public life on earth. Too often, we fall.

(5<sup>th</sup> Mysteries) As Jesus hung dying on the cross [Sorrowful], He gave His Mother to John as our mother, too. In humility and love for Our Lord, we woefully share in this by keeping open a connection to Jesus and His Father through constant prayer [Loveful]. His mother has repeatedly asked that of us. Jesus prayed to His father on the cross as He had also done in the Garden of Gethsemane. Praying and keeping His commandments are how we stay close to Jesus.

# CHAPTER THREE

## The Meditation Bead

## THE MEDITATION BEAD

St. Therese of Lisieux, the Little Flower, had trouble saying the Rosary. In her autobiography, *Story of a Soul,* St. Therese said that meditating on the mysteries was difficult. But she didn't give up.

In the same way, regularly praying the Rosary can be difficult for many of us in the beginning. But don't give up. Our spiritual and sometimes even our physical health strengthens when we learn and practice the discipline of the Rosary. Our Lady has consistently asked us to pray the Rosary.

Even when it is difficult (hopefully temporarily) to focus on the Rosary or on prayer generally, it is still better to pray the Rosary than not to pray it at all. In that way, we can maintain the regularity of daily prayer. Otherwise, we can fall into the worse habit of stopping to pray altogether.

Remember that, in addition to the Rosary, there are many other prayers that are available to us, especially including our own personal prayers. We should strive daily to raise our hearts and minds to God.

Should we enter a time of "spiritual dryness," we should do what saints have done: continue doing what we had been doing before, or what we know we should have been doing. Don't give up on prayer.

Don't give up.

•••••••••

A Meditation Bead is unique. It is a quiet bead. However, like everything else, they're optional.

Many people who have trouble concentrating through an entire Rosary may find them helpful. Some might also find them helpful in setting aside a short pause in silence to find an extra connection with God.

Some people may be able to make or modify their own rosaries to add a Meditation Bead in each decade. That can happen in rosary-making classes or through one's own resources.

Meditation Beads are placed exactly in the middle of each

decade, between the 5<sup>th</sup> and 6<sup>th</sup> Hail Mary beads. This means that there will be five additional beads in a five-decade rosary. These beads should be selected so as not to distract or be confused with the separate and (hopefully) larger Our Father beads.

It is recommended that they be sized differently from the surrounding Hail Mary beads. Generally, they should be smaller so they can be easily identified — and not confused with the Our Father beads — or one will wrongly think the decade is finished.

They can also benefit by being a different texture so that the fingers will have no trouble telling them apart from the adjoining Hail Mary beads.

To further differentiate them from the Our Father beads, there should be no additional spacing on each side, only what is needed for the placement of the bead. Generally, that will be the same spacing as between the Hail Mary beads.

Ensure that Meditation Beads are carefully selected and placed. After regularly using them for a while, you should not confuse them with the other beads.

As a further help, Our Father beads should also be distinctive. When possible, they should be noticeably larger than the Hail Mary beads. To make them cheaper and more quickly, many rosary makers use beads that are all the same size. That's too bad, but such rosaries work anyway.

*In the above photo, a Meditation Bead is at the left side. Note the bead's smaller size and different texture. In this rosary, it is difficult to confuse it with the much larger Our Father bead at the right.*

*Another Meditation Bead.*

*Meditation Beads can come in different shapes. This one is oblong.*

*This rosary has five Meditation Beads.*

*This is an example of an improvised Meditation Bead. This one is made of some easy-to-find Teflon pipe sealing tape wrapped in the middle of the decade. For a distinctive texture, it has a short length of string tied on top of it.*

If one wants to use a Meditation Bead but can't add an actual bead, multiple layers of a narrow piece of utility tape, perhaps with a piece of string tied on top, can be placed at the center of each decade. One can also consider using other materials.

As noted below, the object of these beads is to have something the fingers can feel to remind the person to focus on the mystery or prayers in case the mind has drifted, as many do. When the bead — or a makeshift bead — is felt with the fingers, but meditation and prayers are already proceeding from the heart, just skip by it.

Nonetheless, some might want to stop and use them for an extended period of spiritual silence or meditation before completing the decade.

How important is silence? In part, St. John Paul II wrote this:

*Listening and meditation are nourished by silence. After the announcement of the mystery and the proclamation of the word, it is fitting to pause and focus one's attention for a suitable period of time on the mystery concerned, before moving into vocal prayer.*[42]

Although St. John Paul II described a silence at the beginning of the decade, an ongoing meditation on each Rosary mystery

---

[42] *From the* Apostolic Letter, Rosarium Virginis Mariae Of The Supreme Pontiff John Paul II, *Chapter Three (31), October 16, 2002.*

is also important. In a public setting, the Meditation Bead offers a second opportunity within each decade to pause for reflection.

One might pause on each Meditation Bead in silence, perhaps for 15 or 20 seconds, before moving on. One can also simply take a deep cleansing breath at the bead and then move on to immediately finish the decade. At a minimum, one should simply repeat the mystery to bring it to mind again.

Meditation beads are optional. Many might find them helpful. Others may not.

As mentioned, the primary purpose of this bead is its most important. While saying the Rosary, it is not unusual for some people to begin to daydream or become rote, repeating the prayers without thinking and with no concentration on either the mysteries or the prayers themselves. This is especially true towards the second half of each decade.

This bead is a tool to fight a lack of mental or spiritual discipline, a reminder and opportunity to bring wandering minds back to the mystery of the decade.

There is also help in other places for those whose attention might drift while praying. At times, it certainly happens to all of us. Fortunately, Meditation Beads can be a particularly valuable help.

However, Meditation Beads will only work if you want them to work, if you consciously want to regain or strengthen spiritual discipline in prayer. For some people, it can be an aid to do that. But you have to use it. Otherwise, you can daydream right through that bead, too.

The Meditation Bead is at a point in each decade at which one can take a spiritual breath, slowing the pace for a brief moment, calming down in the peace of prayer before finishing the decade.

This should not suggest that the Rosary is a drudgery with which we struggle. With regular prayer, it should become quite the opposite. But we must also recognize that distractions and human failings in most of us can distract from what should be the richness of a peaceful or meditative frame of mind. That should be integral as we pray the Rosary.

The Meditation Bead can also allow us more time to quietly consider other aspects of the mystery of that decade. This does not mean that one has not already been meditating on the mystery. That should be an ongoing process throughout each decade. But it does allow an extra moment that might permit a slightly more complex consideration of the mystery — its meaning to Jesus, to Our Lady, and to ourselves.

It allows us to take that important spiritual breath mid-decade, or to capture an additional quiet moment for extra contemplation — but only if needed. Otherwise, one should simply move through it without pausing at all.

As those praying become more comfortable with — and not distracted by — silence in their hearts, they might pause longer, as long as the connection with God is strong or as long as the additional concentration on the mystery is productive. There is no limit here.

Note that when praying the Chaplet of the Divine Mercy, for example, the Meditation Bead should be passed over without pause so as not to distract from the rhythm of the chaplet.

If the bead itself should ever prove to be an unhelpful distraction, it's easy to just skip by it — and that should be done — or use a rosary without these beads.

Public Rosaries: If using the Meditation Bead when saying the Rosary with a group of people, the leader can simply say something like, "Let us pause to meditate on [name the mystery]" and then pause for perhaps 10 to 15 seconds. For a group already familiar with using Meditation Beads, a leader can simply announce "Meditation Bead" and allow a standard, short time for reflection — or just skip it entirely.

Since public or group Rosaries rarely have quality additional time to meditate on mysteries, a moment of meditation in each decade may be the only time that can be put aside for it. Each person may want to focus on a particular thought or inspiration from the decade that will serve them best.

Leaders should generally refrain from the temptation to fill in the silence with the noise of their own meditations on the mystery. It is meant as a short time of quiet reflection within each person, for each person's thoughts on the mystery as it relates to them.

On the other hand, there may indeed be times when someone can voice short, careful, and appropriate meditations at each Meditation Bead in a group Rosary. But the primary purpose for the Meditation Bead remains a short time of quiet personal reflection and spiritual refreshment before continuing. (Hopefully, such reflection won't include wondering about some text or email that just arrived.)

However, in group Rosary settings today, it may be best to simply skip through them without pause since most people aren't yet familiar with them and don't have them in their rosaries. Time and attention are often limited in public Rosaries; skipping these beads is often practical.

•••••••••

On September 2, 2016, in Medjugorje, Our Lady said that she "...will teach [us that] to love and to pray [to Her Son, Jesus] means to pray in the silence of [our] soul and not only reciting with [our] lips."

One month later, on October 2, 2016, Our Lady said, "In the silence of your heart, listen to the voice of my Son, so that your heart may be His home, that it may not be dark and sad, but that it may be illuminated with the light of my Son."

These are not the first times Our Lady has mentioned the importance of silence when speaking of prayer.

When Our Lady repeats the same lesson to us, it is usually a lesson that she wants us to learn. Just thirty days apart, Our Lady asked us to both pray in the silence of our soul and to listen to her Son "in the silence of our heart."

So, twice in short order, Our Lady said that we should both pray and be open to listening to her Son by developing the spiritual discipline of silence.

Catholics already know the value of silence. Over the centuries, some cloistered religious communities have kept vows of silence as they endeavor to become and remain close to God and to better know His will. The best retreats have long been silent retreats. An appropriate fast often accompanies quiet prayer in our hearts.

Although silence in the Rosary is often used to meditate on the mystery, it can also simply be a sacred silence to feel a closeness to God.

The Meditation Bead allows us to take a small step on the way to do this.

As you use rosaries with these additional beads, some might begin to look forward to the peace they can bring, to the break in a decade that allows us to regain control of our thoughts.

We are told that St. Dominic felt that prayer *"must include the silent consciousness of the divine Presence."* We also hear that St. Dominic *"added to this simplest of prayers the practice of quiet and silence."*[43]

When the Rosary is said aloud, there are often just two times when one can give special attention to meditating on the mystery of the decade: before the prayers of the decade begin, and at the Meditation Bead.

Regardless of how the Rosary is prayed, the Meditation Bead can become another tool in our connection to God and Our Lady. It can become a moment of spiritual refreshment. Perhaps we add a special personal prayer at that moment. Nonetheless, nothing should be forced or required. It is a spiritual moment of pause only. The Rosary itself, with its meditations on the mysteries, remains primary.

After those few seconds, we continue with the decade. We continue meditating on the mystery and the prayers. We contemplate the desires of Jesus and Our Lady for us and for the world.

In the added spirituality and discipline of the Meditation Bead, we might experience an increased awareness of our own need for spiritual growth. It takes spiritual, even physical discipline to keep focused on prayer. If a Meditation Bead can help us to do that, it is valuable. If it does not, it should be skipped without pause.

Regardless of the presence or absence of a Meditation Bead, we should strive to more strongly sense and understand that God is all around us — that He is actually talking to us — if only we would listen.

When ordering a rosary, ask whether the manufacturer of the rosary can add these beads. If you attend a rosary-making class, you can add them yourself. If neither is available, you

---

[43] *As per* The Life of Saint Dominic *by Bede Jarrett, O.P. Evidence of this actually referring to the Rosary is not available to the author. (See the earlier History of the Rosary.*

can try adding something to let your fingers know when they come up.

But, as mentioned, use them only if they are helpful in your prayers.

# CHAPTER FOUR

## Rosary Connections

# THE ROSARY'S UNSEEN STRUCTURE

This final chapter considers the Rosary's framework, structure, and connections. The observations here serve as further evidence of both the complexity and simplicity of the Rosary.

## THE 3/2 SPLIT

Each of the five sets of Rosary mysteries can be split into two groups of related mysteries: the first three and the last two mysteries. We'll look at each set, how these frameworks might connect to each other, with additional thoughts on some of the mysteries.

### THE JOYFUL MYSTERIES.

The first three Joyful Mysteries all relate to one topic: The Nativity — the Birth of Jesus.

The *1st Joyful Mystery* relates to the conception of Jesus, the first step on the way to His birth. The angel Gabriel tells Mary that she will conceive and bear a son who will be called "Son of the Most High." Mary responds, *"Behold, I am the servant of the Lord."* [Luke 1:31-32, 38.]

*The 2nd Joyful Mystery* is The Visitation. Mary visits her cousin, Elizabeth, who will soon be the mother of John the Baptist. It might seem as though the 2nd Joyful Mystery simply remembers Mary's caring visit to her cousin. But there is more to this.

The angel Gabriel told Mary that Elizabeth was in her sixth month of pregnancy (Luke 1:36). Mary then stayed with her cousin for three months (Luke 1:56). That means that Mary likely stayed with Elizabeth until at least the time of John's birth since that would have been the ninth month of pregnancy for Elizabeth.

If Mary had delayed for even a short time preparing for her journey to visit Elizabeth,[44] she would almost assuredly have been there not only for the birth of John the Baptist, but

---

[44] *In Luke 1:39, we are told that Mary went to her cousin "in haste."*

possibly for a short time thereafter before finally returning home. After all, would Mary have left her cousin at the critical time at the end of Elizabeth's pregnancy? I am doubtful that Mary would have done that.[45]

But what is really happening during all of this time?

*Mary is pregnant.*

Mary's pregnancy and her visit to her cousin is the next part of the journey on the way to Jesus's birth. Does Mary sit home, nervous and babying herself? (It is generally assumed that it was not a difficult pregnancy.) She does not. She goes to help her cousin who was "in her old age" and who was even further along in her pregnancy. She may have also helped Elizabeth care for her husband, Zechariah. (At the time, Zechariah could not speak.)

When Mary finally left Elizabeth, possibly after the birth of John the Baptist, she may have been in her third or fourth month of pregnancy.

So far, we have conception and now an extended moment in Mary's pregnancy.

Finally, *the 3rd Joyful Mystery* is the birth itself. *The first two mysteries have led to this*. It is the culmination of the previous two Joyful Mysteries. All are linked together.

———

Now we look at the final two Joyful Mysteries. These have a slightly different focus. Jesus has already been born. So we might look at the 4th and 5th Joyful Mysteries as representing Jesus growing up. He is still an infant during the Presentation in the Temple.

In the 5th Joyful Mystery, Jesus is 12-years-old when He is found *"in the Temple, where he was sitting among the teachers, listening to them and asking them questions. And all who heard him were amazed at his intelligence and his answers."* He had failed to accompany his parents when they

---

[45] *If she had actually stayed long enough after the birth of John the Baptist, Mary might even have personally witnessed Zechariah regaining his speech after he wrote that his son's name would be John. "Immediately, his mouth was opened and his tongue was freed, and he began to speak, giving praise to God," [Luke 1:64]. Mary would certainly have remembered that as they named Jesus.*

separately left Jerusalem to travel home. [Luke 2:42-49.]

*An Aside:* Some people wrongly think that, by asking questions of the teachers in the Temple, Jesus was endeavoring to learn from them. Quite the opposite. Whether through the Socratic Method of questioning or in its use by competent university professors, *the art of asking questions is skillfully employed by a questioner — to teach the listener.* At 12-years-old, Jesus asked questions of the teachers. Jesus was instructing the teachers. His answers to their questions completed the circle in that, whether asking or answering, at 12-years-old, Jesus knew Jewish Law in light of God's law and the history of creation beyond what any of his listeners would ever know. It is no wonder that *"all who heard him were amazed at his intelligence and his answers."* [Luke 2:47.]

The first three mysteries directly relate to the Nativity culminating in the Divine Birth. The last two mysteries briefly relate to Jesus growing up. The first three mysteries are together. So are the last two.

### THE LUMINOUS MYSTERIES.

The *1st Luminous Mystery* is the very *public* Baptism of Jesus by John the Baptist at the river Jordan. Jesus's Father announces, *"You are my beloved Son; in you I am well pleased."* (Mark 1:11.)

The *2nd Luminous Mystery* is the first public miracle by Jesus at the Wedding Feast at Cana. His mother asks her son to help because the wine has run out. Although we can't know for sure, Mary's asking suggests to the author (but apparently to few others) that Mary would have already seen an unknown number of miracles in her family before that moment. Otherwise, why would Mary have suggested to Jesus, with confidence, that He could fix the problem?

Dueling theologians interpret this event differently. Yet, regardless of other interpretations, the author feels that Mary must have already seen the power of her Son, privately, as He was growing up.

Although His divine wisdom had been seen publicly in the

Temple at 12 years of age, this was the scriptural moment of His first public miracle. Others then knew what Jesus could do.[46]

Finally, *the 3rd Luminous Mystery,* the Proclamation of the Kingdom, couldn't have been more public. Jesus preached to thousands of people. It was the teaching foundation of Christianity, waiting for nothing further than Jesus's later death and resurrection.

Those are the first three very public Luminous Mysteries.

———

The 4th and 5th Luminous Mysteries change. Both events in these mysteries are done in *private.*

In the 4th Luminous Mystery, the Transfiguration, Jesus takes just three disciples with Him: Peter, James, and John (Mark 9:2-8).

The 5th Luminous Mystery is the Institution of the Eucharist. Note that Jesus did not give the Eucharist to the world, but only to His closest disciples who believed in Him. It was done in an upper room, away from the public. He didn't institute the Eucharist in front of a large crowd. (Other than Judas,) only select believers who loved and respected the Lord were there.

The first three Luminous Mysteries tell of events that happened in *public.* The last two mysteries were clearly *private* events. The first three mysteries are together, as are the last two.

## THE SORROWFUL MYSTERIES.

The Passion of Jesus stands apart from other mysteries. Is there anything that unites these mysteries? The sufferings of Our Lord in the first three mysteries are His sufferings in preparation for the Cross. In contrast, the last two mysteries are directly connected to His crucifixion. Nonetheless, it is more difficult to identify the same structure in the Passion of Jesus as it is in other mysteries.

———

---

[46] *Note that Jesus already had disciples at the time who were present for this miracle [John 2: 2, 11-12].*

However, the last two Sorrowful Mysteries clearly do have something in common: The Cross.

Jesus carries the Cross. He is then put to death on the Cross.

So the final two Sorrowful Mysteries are connected, sharing something in common — as do the 4th and 5th mysteries in all other sets of mysteries. Meditation might suggest further distinctions and connections. In truth, the Passion is inseparable. It stands together as one event. Nonetheless, we will briefly look at its 3$^{rd}$ mystery in the coming section on the pinnacle mysteries.

## THE LOVEFUL MYSTERIES.

The first three Loveful Mysteries are straightforward. Their focus is entirely on love.

The *1st Loveful Mystery* reminds us that there is no greater love than to lay down one's life for a friend. Following the Sorrowful Mysteries, the connection is obvious. This is what Jesus did for sinners. This is what martyrs have often done for others. It should not surprise people that many of us might also do the same thing should a threat to another call for it. There is "no greater love."

The *2nd Loveful Mystery* is both a teaching and a goal for love in our daily lives: whatever we do for others, we do for Jesus, Our Lord. There are often opportunities for love that we might see, but on which we fail to act. Are we called to love everyone? Are there limits? This is something worthy of discussion and meditation.

Finally, the *3rd Loveful Mystery* lays before us the Greatest Commandment. It then follows up with the second.

*"'You shall love the Lord your God with all your heart, and with all your soul, and with all your mind.' This is the greatest and the first commandment. The second is like it: 'You shall love your neighbor as yourself.' Everything in the Law and the Prophets depends on these two commandments."* [Matthew 22:36-40.]

Again, this is framed as a commandment, not merely an aspiration or suggestion. How can we do this? It is our goal. It is what Jesus has told us to do. It is what we *must* do. But, like so much else, it's not always easy. A pious life with prayer consistently bring us closer to that love. We can do this.

———

The 4th and 5th Loveful Mysteries change from direct talk of love to less direct but essential tools to develop even more love within us — especially through prayer.

The 4th Loveful Mystery, The Beatitudes, opens up many opportunities for meditations as we pray this mystery of the Rosary. One does not have to consider every Beatitude every time. Reflecting on one or two each time can be beneficial. We can also look at the Beatitudes as a concrete symbol and reminder of *all* the teachings that Jesus has given us.

Prayer is often said to be two-way: we talk; we listen. Does not the 4th mystery suggest that we should be earnestly listening as Jesus speaks to us in Scripture? That is not restricted to the Sermon on the Mount: the Beatitudes. It includes teachings throughout Scripture.

The 5th Loveful Mystery, Pray Without Ceasing, tells us that we should make our life a prayer. It tells us that we should be constantly aware of God throughout the day, even if we're not formally praying. We spent much time talking about this earlier. Love is often part of prayer from the heart.

The first three mysteries relate directly to Love: what it is, what we can actively do, and the Greatest Commandment. The last two mysteries relate to prayer along with meditations on Jesus's teachings, which we might take as part of prayerful listening. The first three mysteries are together. So are the last two.

## THE GLORIOUS MYSTERIES.

Finally, we consider the clearest example of the separation between the first three and last two mysteries: The Glorious Mysteries.

The *1st Glorious Mystery,* the Resurrection, is foundational to Christianity. Most believe that the term "Christian" cannot even be applied to those who deny the Resurrection.

The *2nd Glorious Mystery,* the Ascension, finally ends Jesus's active teaching while with us on earth. His time from birth through the Ascension has set in motion the whole of

Christianity during the past two millennia.

The *3rd Glorious Mystery,* The Descent of the Holy Spirit Upon the Apostles, gave wisdom and strength to the apostles to spread the message of salvation throughout the world. It gives them the courage they will later need to lay down their lives for Christ. Before He left them, Jesus told His disciples that the Holy Spirit would come. These first three mysteries are supernatural events that show the power and majesty of God.

———

But then, although still reflecting the power of God, things change. The 4th Glorious Mystery, the Assumption, recalls the bodily assumption of Mary into heaven. This is generally not considered to be specifically found in Scripture. However, although one has always been able to find doubters, this has long been believed by Christians. It was only when persistent doubt continued centuries later that the Catholic Church formally defined it as dogma.

The 5th Glorious Mystery, the Crowning of Our Lady as Queen of Heaven and Earth, is also not explicitly found in Scripture. Nonetheless, it has been supported by private revelation over the centuries and has long been accepted by Catholics.

The first three mysteries relate directly to the supernatural events as Jesus ended his time on earth. The last two mysteries relate directly to Mary. The first three mysteries are together. So are the last two.[47]

---

[47] *Note that even the reportedly original fourth and fifth Glorious Mysteries, as noted earlier in the book, would be linked together:* The Second Coming *and* The General Judgment.

# THE PINNACLE MYSTERIES

Consider that the third mysteries can be looked at as "pinnacle mysteries." Although every mystery of the Rosary is important, it can be argued that these mysteries may have some special importance within each set of mysteries.

Is this to say that the pinnacle mysteries are more important than other mysteries in each set of Rosary mysteries? Not necessarily.

Meditate on the pinnacle mysteries alone, but also meditate in continuity with the mysteries which precede them.

In her excellent book, *Mary: A History of Doctrine and Devotion* (1963/2009), Hilda Graef wrote:

*"The most important moment in the life of the nascent Church [was] when the Apostles are waiting for the outpouring of the Spirit at Pentecost."*

I'm not saying, as just one example, that the Descent of the Holy Spirit is more important than the Resurrection! But I am saying that the first and second mysteries appear to build towards the pinnacle third mystery in each set of mysteries.

The simple list of the five "pinnacle" mysteries includes:

> The Birth of Jesus;
> The Proclamation of the Kingdom of God;
> The Crowning with Thorns;
> The Greatest Commandment;
> The Descent of the Holy Spirit Upon the Apostles.

Although I won't present the case for each one here, I will mention one.

•••••••••

Few people truly understand the extent of suffering brought about by the crown of thorns. Medical researchers who have written about it will enlighten readers as to the horrendous suffering Jesus endured with this "crown." It was almost assuredly not the simple circle of thorns around the top of the head which is often depicted in art. Instead, it is considered to have been a pileus. That is a cap which covers much of the head. Here, it would have been lined with particularly painful thorns along the inside. Even the Shroud of Turin supports this type of "crown."

The terrible and more dramatic scourging is considered to be worse by many people because its suffering is easier to picture, as was seen in the 2004 movie, The Passion of the Christ. The scourging was horrendous, but the extent of pain caused by the crown of thorns is rarely fully understood and is, therefore, often overlooked.

A number of sources present compelling evidence of the terrible suffering inflicted by the crown of thorns. The result of this torture, combined with the scourging, most likely led to the unexpectedly faster death of Jesus on the Cross.[48]

---

[48] *See* What Christ Suffered *by Thomas W. McGovern, M.D.;* The Crucifixion of Jesus: A Forensic Inquiry *by Frederick T. Zugibe, M.D., Ph.D., as well as the older* A Doctor at Calvary *by Dr. Pierre Barbet, along with other good sources for specific details on the sufferings of Jesus.*

## INTRA-ROSARY CONNECTIONS

Certain other intra-Rosary connections appear to exist. I'll briefly mention some of these as observed in the first, second, and fourth mysteries.

The third mysteries connect as pinnacle mysteries. The fifth mysteries connect more subtly and are not mentioned here.

**Within the first mysteries,** we find one or more of three things together: **(#1)** Demonstrations of humility or submission; **(#2)** Supernatural events; and/or **(#3)** The presence of a Person of the Trinity as part of that supernatural event. Only the first mysteries of the Joyful and Luminous Mysteries appear to have all three.

The first Joyful Mystery sees Mary humbly submitting to the will of God [#1: a demonstration of humility and submission] as she responds to the coming of the angel Gabriel [#2: a supernatural event]. *"Behold, I am the handmaid of the Lord. May it be done to me according to your word."* Luke 1:38.

Mary's humility to God opens the door so that Jesus might be *"conceived by the Holy Spirit."* (*"The Holy Spirit will come upon you, and the power of the Most High will overshadow you."* Luke 1:35.) [#3: a presence of two persons of the Trinity: the Holy Spirit & Jesus, conceived.]

The first Luminous Mystery sees Jesus asking to be baptized (in submission to John the Baptist, as#1, above). John the Baptist said that it was he who should be baptized by Jesus. Jesus insisted, and John baptized Him. After He was baptized, a supernatural event occurred (see #2, above):

> *"...The heavens were opened... and he saw the Spirit of God descending like a dove [and] coming upon him."* (Matthew 3:16.)

The presence of God the Father, the First Person of the Blessed Trinity (see #3, above), is heard by those present in a voice from heaven: *"This is my beloved Son, with whom I am well pleased."* (Matthew 3:17.)

The first Sorrowful Mystery is the Agony in the Garden. Jesus prays to His Father: *"Father, if you are willing, take this cup away from me; still, not my will but yours be done (#1)."* (Luke 22:42.) While he is praying, an angel appears to Him (#2) to give Him strength. (Luke 22:43.) Jesus submits to His Father's will. On the coming day, He will suffer and die for our sins.

The first Loveful Mystery is not an event. However, (#1) laying down one's life for another is the greatest act of submission in love. This mystery recalls Jesus's words: There is No Greater Love. (John 15:13.)

The first Glorious Mystery is the Resurrection (#2). Jesus, the Second Person of the Blessed Trinity (#3), has risen from the dead.

**The second mysteries** appear to have subtleties in common. They are generally not private events, most involve service to another, and they are transitional between the first and third mysteries:

The second Joyful Mystery of the Visitation is a transition from the Annunciation to the birth of Jesus. Elizabeth was the only person who could understand Mary's miraculous conception because, although not a conception by the Holy Spirit as with Mary, Elizabeth's pregnancy was also a special gift from God. Besides being a help to Elizabeth, Mary would feel safe with her. This mystery shows Mary giving herself *in service* to another person, to her cousin, Elizabeth.

The second Luminous Mystery of the Wedding Feast at Cana transitions from a private life to one of public miracles. The public miracle at Cana shows Jesus in service to others — not simply to those at the wedding, but to His mother as He responds to her request.

The second Sorrowful Mystery transitions from the dread of

what is coming in the first mystery, through the scourging, to what some may consider to have been even greater suffering with the Crown of Thorns. Jesus gives Himself in what goes far beyond mere service as His suffering takes away our sins. It is the sacrifice and love of Jesus beyond our understanding. It awaits the thorns and the cross.

The second Loveful Mystery transitions from sacrifice, of which there is No Greater Love, to a teaching about our own love in earthly service to others — and to Jesus through the others whom we serve. By helping us to grow in love through actions in our daily lives, this mystery then transitions us to the third mystery, the Greatest Commandment: *"To love the Lord, your God, with all your heart, with all your soul, and with all your mind,"* and to *"Love your neighbor as yourself."*

The second Glorious Mystery — the Ascension of Jesus into Heaven — differs from the Resurrection. No one saw the Resurrection. Witnesses arrived at the tomb and saw that it was empty. By contrast, His disciples openly witness Jesus ascend into heaven. Jesus told His disciples to stay in the city to await the gift of the Holy Spirit. He knows that He will no longer be physically there for them. This mystery is transitional because only after He ascends does the Holy Spirit come to fill the hearts of His apostles (Luke 24:49).

**The fourth mysteries** are transitional, in most cases to the fifth mysteries.

The fourth Joyful Mystery, the Presentation, transitions from Jesus being an infant in the fourth mystery to an older but still young Jesus when He is found at the temple in the fifth Joyful Mystery.

The fourth Luminous Mystery is transitional from Jesus being seen as human by His apostles in their day-to-day lives — though they knew He was more than that — to seeing Him in the totally supernatural event of the Transfiguration. This may be part of an even greater supernatural transition from what His apostles had known to something beyond. Jesus was both God and Man.

Carrying the cross in the fourth Sorrowful Mystery leads to Jesus's death on the cross in the fifth mystery.

The fourth Loveful Mystery may be considered a subset of the broader fifth mystery of prayer and the understandings gained through prayer. (Loveful Mysteries are teachings, not events.)

In the fourth Glorious Mystery, Mary's Assumption is transitional to her being crowned Queen of Heaven and Earth in the fifth Glorious Mystery.

Any awareness of conjectured structures while praying the Rosary should not distract us from the prayer itself. Nonetheless, the numerous connections and transitions further connect us to the complex and powerful prayer that is the Rosary. They are food for meditation.

In *The Excellence of the Rosary,* we read this:

*"The Rosary in its union of vocal prayer and meditation is a perfect prayer."*[49]

Pray the Rosary.

---

[49] *From* The Excellence of the Rosary (1912) *by Reverend M.J. Frings (reprinted by Refuge of Sinners Publishing in 2019).*

Some may wish to memorize one of the following or another appropriate prayer.

## A PRAYER FOR LOVE

Father in Heaven, You who is love... loving and merciful Jesus, my Lord... Holy Spirit who gives me the courage, wisdom, and strength to put love into noble action in the world, and to love God above all, graciously increase your love within me. May I be its reflection for others that they may also love you. May it be an impenetrable armor to protect me and all of us from Satan, whose work it is to destroy heavenly love in each of us and in the world.

Grant me your mercy for my failings and instill your peace within me forever. As my help and joy, may my heart, my voice, and my life always be raised to you in prayer. Graciously watch over me and over all of us who long to endure as your children, though, so often, imperfect ones. In your mercy and caring, please protect us and love us all in this life and in the life to come. Amen.

## (2) A SHORTER VERSION OF THIS PRAYER

Most loving God, graciously increase your love within us. May we be its reflection for others that they may also love you. May your love be our armor to protect us from evil. Grant us your mercy for our failings and instill your peace within us. Please protect and love us all in this life and in the life to come. Amen.

## (3) THE SHORTEST VERSION

Most loving God, graciously increase your love and peace within us. Grant us your mercy for our failings. Please protect and love us in this life and in the life to come. Amen.

And please pray for me, too.

# APPENDICES

## APPENDIX A:
## THE MYSTERIES OF THE ROSARY

Here are the mysteries of the Rosary as a review or reference. They're listed in order of the chronology of the life of Jesus and Mary. Note that this is not the order in which one says the mysteries when saying just five decades a day as per the current daily schedule for the mysteries. Also included here are the Loveful Mysteries whose chronology is different since they are predominantly based on teachings, not events. A small booklet is also available called, *"The Loveful Mysteries of the Rosary"* presenting a small part of this book.

### Joyful Mysteries
Mondays.
[Note: If the Loveful Mysteries are not prayed, the Joyful Mysteries are said on Mondays and Saturdays.]

(1)     The Annunciation;
(2)     The Visitation;
(3)     The Birth of Jesus;
(4)     The Presentation;
(5)     The Finding of Jesus in the Temple.

\* \* \*

### Luminous Mysteries
(also called the Mysteries of Light)
Thursdays.

(1)     The Baptism of Jesus in the Jordan;
(2)     Jesus's Self-Manifestation at the Wedding
of Cana;
(3)     The Proclamation of the Kingdom of God;
(4)     The Transfiguration;
(5)     The Institution of the Eucharist.

\* \* \*

## Loveful Mysteries
Saturdays;
Tuesdays, together with the Sorrowful Mysteries.

(1)   No Greater Love;
(2)   Whatever You Do For One (You Do For Me);
(3)   The Greatest Commandment;
(4)   The Beatitudes;
(5)   Pray Without Ceasing.

\* \* \*

## Sorrowful Mysteries
Fridays;
Tuesdays (with or without the Loveful Mysteries).

(1)   The Agony in the Garden;
(2)   The Scourging at the Pillar;
(3)   The Crowning with Thorns;
(4)   The Carrying of the Cross;
(5)   The Crucifixion.

\* \* \*

## Glorious Mysteries
Wednesdays; Sundays.

(1)   The Resurrection;
(2)   The Ascension;
(3)   The Descent of the Holy Spirit Upon the Apostles;
(4)   The Assumption;
(5)   The Crowning of Our Lady as Queen of Heaven and Earth.

\* \* \*

On Sundays of Advent and Christmas, the Joyful Mysteries are said. On Sundays in Lent, the Sorrowful Mysteries are said. The author recommends adding the Chaplet of the Divine Mercy after praying a Rosary. Of course, the Divine Mercy Chaplet can also be prayed entirely separately.

## APPENDIX B:
## HOW TO PRAY THE ROSARY

(1) Hold the crucifix (or cross) on the rosary while making the Sign of the Cross. Consider for which intention you would like to offer the Rosary. Then say the Apostles Creed.[50]

(2) The first bead after the crucifix (or cross) is the first Our Father. The Our Father bead is always surrounded by extra spacing to separate it from the Hail Mary beads. On some rosaries, the Our Father bead is a larger bead which makes it easier to identify with the fingers. Larger Our Father beads are helpful but not necessary. Say the Our Father on these beads. Counting the opening Our Father, there are six Our Fathers in a five-decade Rosary.

(3) Following the Our Father bead at the beginning of the rosary are three Hail Mary beads spaced more closely together. The intentions for these three early Hail Mary beads are, respectively, for Faith, Hope, and Charity (love). While not required, it is good to announce those intentions prior to saying their respective Hail Marys. Then say the Hail Mary on these three early beads. There are 53 Hail Marys in a five-decade Rosary.

(4) Move your fingers to the space immediately following the last of those first three Hail Mary's. Say the Glory Be prayer in that space. Then say the Fatima Prayer. There are slightly different forms of this prayer, but they all work:

> *"Oh [my] Jesus, forgive us our sins, save us from the fires of hell, [and] lead all souls to heaven, especially those in most need of Thy mercy."*

Although some still refer to it as optional, the Fatima Prayer is almost universally said. It has effectively become an integral part of the Rosary. Our Lady gave the prayer to the visionaries

---

[50] *Local customs or other sects in the world might replace the Apostles Creed or other Rosary prayers with different ones.*

at Fatima on July 13, 1917.

Some might look at the Divine Mercy as a response to this prayer. The author believes that it is.

(5) The next bead is the next Our Father, a separated bead. Before beginning the Our Father, say (or announce, if the Rosary is said with others) the appropriate Rosary mystery. (See the Mysteries of the Rosary listed earlier.) Then say the Our Father on this bead.

(6) Next are ten Hail Marys. As you say them, try to meditate on various aspects of the mystery that you announced before the Our Father as the decade began. Later in this book, you will learn about optional Meditation Beads in the middle of the ten Hail Marys.

(7) When the ten Hail Marys are finished, complete the decade by saying the Glory Be and Fatima prayers in the space before the next Our Father.

(8) After finishing the first decade, continue with the next four decades in the same way.

(9) At the end of the Rosary, say the Hail Holy Queen prayer. Although it is a separate prayer, in most places it is considered and taught as part of the Rosary. Most practicing Catholics know — or should know — this prayer. (Memorize it if you don't.)

(10) That should be followed by a final prayer after the Rosary, although far fewer people have memorized this prayer:

*[Let us pray.] O God, whose only begotten Son, by His life, death, and resurrection, has purchased for us the rewards of eternal life, grant, we beseech Thee, that meditating upon these mysteries of the Most Holy Rosary of the Blessed Virgin Mary, we may imitate what they contain and obtain what they promise, through the same Christ Our Lord. Amen.*

(11) Beyond that, there are many prayers that can be added at your discretion. You can also finish without adding anything else. The prayer to St. Michael used to be more common than it is today, but is often still said. It is good to add it. In addition, you might consider memorizing and adding a *Prayer for Love* found earlier in the *Closing Prayers*. You can also add short pious invocations to the Sacred Heart or to favorite saints, as many as you like — or add other prayers.

(12) Finish with the Sign of the Cross.

(13) If you go on to say other mysteries, it is not necessary to say the prayers at the end of the Rosary (until you actually finish) nor to say the prayers at the beginning of the Rosary again. Just continue with the next mysteries that you want to pray. When done, you can then say the prayers at the end of the Rosary.

(14) Adding the Divine Mercy Chaplet is recommended. The Chaplet is said using the rosary beads. If you're not familiar with the Chaplet, you can easily find information about it online and at many parish churches. You can also learn the story of St. Faustina and the Chaplet of the Divine Mercy in books and documentary videos. Especially go to the website of the *Marians of the Immaculate Conception* at www.marian.org.

## APPENDIX C:
## PRAYERS OF THE ROSARY.
[Words in brackets are alternative wordings used by many people.]

### The Apostles' Creed
I believe in God, the Father almighty, Creator of heaven and earth, and in Jesus Christ, His only Son, our Lord, Who was conceived by the Holy Spirit, born of the Virgin Mary, suffered under Pontius Pilate, was crucified, died and was buried. He descended into hell; [and] on the third day He rose again from the dead; He ascended into heaven, and is seated at the right hand of God the Father almighty; from there [thence] He will come to judge the living and the dead.

I believe in the Holy Spirit, the holy catholic Church, the communion of saints, the forgiveness of sins, the resurrection of the body, and life everlasting. Amen.
*[Some people still use the old form of* Holy Ghost *instead of* Holy Spirit.*]*

### Our Father
Our Father, who art in heaven, hallowed be Thy name. Thy kingdom come, Thy will be done on earth as it is in heaven. Give us this day our daily bread and forgive us our trespasses as we forgive those who trespass against us. And lead us not into temptation, but deliver us from evil. Amen.

### Hail Mary
Hail Mary, full of grace. The Lord is with thee. Blessed art thou among women, and blessed is the fruit of thy womb, Jesus. Holy Mary, Mother of God, pray for us sinners, now and at the hour of our death. Amen.

### Glory Be
Glory be to the Father, and to the Son, and to the Holy Spirit, as it was in the beginning, is now, and ever shall be, world without end. Amen.

**Oh My Jesus**
Oh [my] Jesus, forgive us our sins, save us from the fires of hell, [and] lead all souls to heaven, especially those in most need of Thy mercy.

**Hail Holy Queen**
Hail Holy Queen, Mother of Mercy, our Life, our Sweetness, and our hope. To thee do we cry, poor banished children of Eve. To thee do we send up our sighs, mourning and weeping in this vale [valley] of tears. Turn then most gracious advocate, thine eyes of mercy toward us, and after this, our exile, show unto us, the blessed fruit of thy womb, Jesus. O clement, O loving, O sweet Virgin Mary. Pray for us O Holy Mother of God, That we may be made worthy of the promises of Christ.

**PRAYER AFTER THE ROSARY [optional]**
*[See* Appendix B *in the previous section.]*

**PRAYER TO ST. MICHAEL [optional]**
Saint Michael, the Archangel, defend us in [this day of] battle; be our safeguard [protection] against the wickedness [malice] and snares of the devil. May God rebuke him, we humbly pray, and do thou [you], O prince of the heavenly host, by the power of God, cast [thrust] into Hell, Satan and all the [other] evil spirits, who prowl [wander] through [about; throughout] the world, seeking the ruin of souls. Amen.
*[You can see that there are a number of alternate wordings for this prayer. There is also an older, much longer version available.]*

**A PRAYER FOR LOVE [optional]**
*[Three options for this prayer are in the Closing Prayers just before the appendix.]*